Music in Cultural Context

Eight Views on World Music Education

PATRICIA SHEHAN CAMPBELL

MUSIC EDUCATORS NATIONAL CONFERENCE

Acknowledgments

I wish to thank the members of the Society for Ethnomusicology's Education Committee for their encouragement and enthusiasm in the planning and execution of the project, particularly Carlesta Henderson-Spearman, Ellen McCullough-Brabson, Jerry Moore, Tony Palmer, Cecilia Riddell, Cliff Sloan, Kari Veblen, Terese Volk, and Edward O'Connor, who compiled the resource list contained at the close of this collection. I am grateful to Miriam Dvorin-Spross for transcribing two of the interviews and to Jeanne Spaeth of the MENC staff for her patience, perseverance, and ever-able editing. My heartfelt appreciation goes to the eight ethnomusicologists who gave of their time to thoughtfully respond to my queries in order that teachers like me might see through their windows to the musical worlds in which they have lived.

Copyright 1996
Music Educators National Conference
1806 Robert Fulton Drive
Reston, VA 20191-4348

Printed in the United States of America
ISBN 1-56545-100-7

CONTENTS

Prelude 1

David P. McAllester on Navajo Music (and Native American music at large) 5

Terry Miller on Thai Music (and Southeast Asian music at large) 12

Bruno Nettl on Music of Iran (and Middle Eastern music at large) 19

Anthony Seeger on Music of Amazonian Indians (particularly music of the Suya) 26

Bell Yung on Music of China (and Chinese music in Hong Kong) 33

Christopher Waterman on Yoruba Music of Africa (and West African music at large) 41

Mellonee Burnim on African American Music (gospel and spirituals) 50

Steven Loza on Latino Music (particularly Mexican and Chicano music) 58

Postlude 66

Resource List *compiled by Edward O'Connor* 72

PRELUDE

The core of this book on "music in cultural context" was first published as a series of interview articles, with sample lessons, in the *Music Educators Journal* from July 1994 through September 1995. These articles are reprinted here under one cover, along with a discussion of issues relevant to the teaching of music as a world and multicultural phenomenon. This introduction, or prelude, briefly argues a rationale for the curricular movement, notes the absence of world music studies from undergraduate programs in music and music education, and recognizes the efforts of professional societies in providing teachers with the means for the development of a knowledge base for teaching more than one musical culture. The Society for Ethnomusicology's Education Committee is described, from which the idea for the "music in cultural context" series first emerged. A framework for the project is described, both by way of its inception and development and through reference to principal issues that arise among teachers in the course of their engagement in teaching musical cultures (which were enveloped in interview questions). An afterword, or postlude, makes note of similar and contradictory views expressed by the eight ethnomusicologists on teaching musics from the cultures of their expertise and from the world at large.

Stretching the Music Curricular Content

World music education is not new to teachers, nor is its counterpart, the heavily invoked curricular practice called "multicultural music education."[1] By the mid-90s, elementary- and secondary-level music educators in general, choral, and, to a lesser extent, instrumental instructors were reflecting in their repertoires the cultural diversity of the American nation and some of the many mother-countries Americans claim as their first homes (or the homes of their ancestors). The recent large influx of immigrants to the United States and the current attention given to individual cultural heritages by American society at large have driven the current use of diverse musical traditions in classrooms and rehearsal halls. Beyond a demographic rationale, however, more than a few music educators are teaching the music of the Vietnamese *cai luong* (theatre), the Indian *bharata natyam* (dance), or the Ewe (Ghana) percussion ensemble sheerly for the beauty and intrigue of the music—music they have selected as worthy of their students' listening attention, participation, and thought. Whatever the perspective, demographic or the purely musical, the music taught and learned in schools spans a much wider spectrum of styles today than it did even a decade ago.

National and state initiatives have provided an important impetus in the search for broader and more varied curricular content—in musical terms, a more diverse musical repertoire. Dimensions of multicultural education are now permeating the curricular philosophies of a large number of school districts. Music, the visual arts, theatre, and movement/dance, along with social studies and language arts, are being held accountable for "content integration," the presentation of information from a variety of cultures to illustrate key concepts and principles.[2] A multicultural approach to subject matter is being upheld by teachers, their administrators, and school boards as a pathway to the reduction of prejudice among students[3] and a means of providing "equity pedagogy" to all students regardless of their racial, ethnic, or social-class group.[4] A small, albeit vocal, group of conservatives warn of a "multicultural mafia" of university professors and lead teachers,[5] who have imposed "ethnocentric, Afrocentric, and bilingual curricula on public schools,"[6] but these charges are not easily validated. Nor have they yet affected the multicultural mandates currently being realized in schools across the country.

University and School Views of the Musical Canon

Yet even as a more expansive view of curriculum is held by music teachers than ever before, there are challenges to be faced in the selection, curricular design, and instructional delivery of these musical worlds to students. Music educators emanate from collegiate teacher education programs that are strongly rooted in ideas and coursework of earlier, Western (largely European) eras. Theory classes, history surveys, ensemble and studio work still attend to music sonorities and structures of the common practice period (the period of eighteenth-century Viennese classicism), the nineteenth-century symphonic, operatic, and chamber music "masterworks" repertoire, and a certain few Romantic-flavored works of the twentieth century. In their four or five years as music majors, prospective teachers all too rarely have opportunities to study and perform works of American composers like Ives and Gershwin or the jazz styles of Count Basie, Miles Davis, and Chick Corea or the musical expressions of long-standing American cultural groups—the sacred harp and shape-note songs of Anglo-Americans, the blues and gospel styles of African Americans, and the social dance songs of Native Americans. As for musics of the world's cultures, most music educators had no exposure in undergraduate studies to the music of Japan, the Zulu of South Africa, Bulgaria, or Indonesia.

A single musical culture, Western European art music, is perpetuated through most collegiate programs in music. Yet upon graduation and placement in their first teaching positions, music educators are confronted with schoolwide missions to teach subjects globally and from a multicultural perspective. The canon of musical works they learned in their undergraduate studies do not often transfer, even in part, to the expectations of school personnel for music repertoire and programs.[7] Principals, parents' groups, and the public at large who press for more culturally diverse curriculum have teachers of music scrambling for music they never learned and songs they never knew. Workshops, clinics, and seminars become important means for learning something of musical cultures with attention to repertoire that is easily accessible and readily learned. Thus, while Western European art music is the common musical language of those trained in American conservatory-styled colleges and universities, it is increasingly viewed by teachers as only one of the many musical cultures (admittedly with its own rich diversity of historical and contemporary styles) to be experienced and learned by students in elementary and public schools.

The Efforts of Professional Societies

Various professional organizations of music teachers are attending to world and multicultural dimensions of music education—among them, the Music Educators National Conference (MENC), the American Choral Directors Association, the American Orff-Schulwerk Association, The College Music Society, the International Society for Music Education, and the Organization of American Kodály Educators. The publications and conference presentations of these societies, particularly in the last fifteen years, show genuine interest in a broadening of musical curricular offerings.[8] The Society for Ethnomusicology's appointment of an Education Committee in 1985 reflected that scholarly profession's growing interest in the interface of ethnomusicology with public sector (including school) populations. The Sonneck Society's attention to American art and vernacular musics and the International Traditional Music Council's emphasis on folk music have relevance to educators, and both groups have formed committees or task forces interested in adapting the findings of scholarly research to curricular practice.

MENC and the Society for Ethnomusicology have a considerable history of collaborations directed toward inspiring teachers in classrooms and rehearsal halls to think and act globally in the selection and delivery of music to students. In 1972, O. M. Hartzell supervised the compilation of "Music in World Cultures," a landmark issue of *Music Educators Journal* devoted to a description of musical traditions and sources. He invited Margaret Mead, anthropologist, and a host of ethnomusicologists to contribute articles on musical traditions from Asia, Africa, the Americas, Europe, and Oceania. Just over a decade later, ethnomusicologist David McAllester collaborated with members of MENC's Interdisciplinary Committee to present the Wesleyan Symposium, a gathering of ethnomusicologists and educators whose focus was music transmission in world cultures. Sponsored by MENC, Wesleyan, and the Theodore Presser Foundation, the symposium's proceedings were published as *Becoming Human through Music* (1984), and included insightful observations of culture-specific approaches to music teaching and learning by scholars such as David McAllester, John Blacking, Adrienne Kaeppler, Bruno Nettl, Tim Rice, and Carol Robertson. MENC's 1989 textbook, *Multicultural Perspectives in Music Education* (with a second edition published in 1996), was still another effort of educators working with ethnomusicologists in recommending sources and procedures for teaching a broader sampling of musical cultures. On the heels of this book, MENC cosponsored with the Smithsonian Institution and the Society for Ethnomusicology the 1990 Symposium on Multicultural Approaches to Music Education, bringing together ethnomusicologists, culture-bearers, and music educators to represent and demonstrate the music of African American, Chinese, Hispanic American (chiefly Cuban/Caribbean and Mexican), and Native American cultures.

The SEM Education Committee

Within the Society for Ethnomusicology (SEM), a "working committee" on music education existed for a short while in the early 1970s, but it was during the presidential terms of John Blacking, Carol Robertson, and Robert Garfias that initiation of the current SEM Education Committee was given serious attention. Upon its inception in 1985, the committee declared its interest in the achievement of four tasks: (1) the identification of cross-cultural materials suitable for classroom use, (2) the creation of publications and settings in which regional resources and specialists could be made known to school systems and interested educators, (3) greater involvement of regional SEM chapters in the needs and resources of educators in different cultural and geographic settings, and (4) increased dialogue between ethnomusicologists and educators, so that clarification can be given to what knowledge is practical and relevant to teaching music from a global perspective. The committee was chaired from 1985 through 1989 by Caroline Card-Wendt and from late 1989 through 1995 by Patricia Shehan Campbell; eight to twelve members constituted the committee, of which the majority were music educators in university and school settings.

In attempting to increase the dialogue between educators and ethnomusicologists, the SEM Education Committee arranged for a presentation by Robert Garfias, then SEM president, at the MENC biennial meeting in Anaheim in 1986. Issues he addressed, and on which discussion ensued, included the possibility of summer workshops in world music for teachers (taught by ethnomusicologists), "resource ethnomusicologists" who could visit collegiate methods classes for preservice music teachers, and resource materials to include visual and audio materials—recordings, videotapes, slides, and the like. About fifty individuals attended the session, many of whom were active in MENC's Multicultural Awareness Commission. Garfias's presentation served as a gateway to a flood of presentations by ethnomusicologists and Education Committee members at succeeding national and regional meetings of MENC and other teachers' organizations. It also inspired the beginning of the "Saturday Morning Education Session" at the annual meeting of the Society, in which the subjects of resources and instructional models have been addressed by ethnomusicologists and educators in workshops, on panels, and through research papers. Depending upon the venue for the meeting, these sessions have drawn as many as two hundred music educators. Sessions at Rochester (1986),

Ann Arbor (1987), Oakland (1990), Chicago (1991), and Milwaukee (1994) were particularly memorable for their unique formats, interactive dialogues, and considerable attendance by area educators.

Beginning in 1990, the SEM Education Committee began the printing of a homespun newsletter. A mailing list of 400 was compiled from participants at the MENC-Smithsonian-SEM Symposium on Multicultural Approaches to Music Education. The list included interested ethnomusicologists, folklorists, and general classroom educators. These newsletters contained announcements of the annual SEM meetings, including topics of the Saturday Morning Education sessions, along with postings of workshops, and new instructional materials on world music/multicultural music education. The newsletters were prepared and sent twice yearly from the University of Washington until early 1993, when budgetary restrictions affected the project. Yet far beyond the newsletter, committee members have been active in "spreading the word" on world music and its parent discipline of ethnomusicology. The current mission statement of the SEM Education Committee reflects the work of its members: "To advance theories and practices of world music education, through sessions at the annual meeting and through work by individual members in other organizations of professional educators. This work includes the presentation of clinical sessions on selected musical cultures, the development of research on transmission/teaching/learning of world music in educational settings, and the publication of position papers and curricular/instructional materials."

The *MEJ* Series

The "music in cultural context" series was one of two projects first discussed at the 1993 meeting of the SEM Education Committee in Oxford, Mississippi. The first of these projects was the development of an annotated bibliography of instructional resources for use by teachers, including recordings (vinyl, tape, and CD) and videotapes. This project was

chaired by Edward O'Connor, professor emeritus at the University of Connecticut, and drafted and revised by him with input from committee members. I outlined the idea for the series project at the meeting and argued that educators could be well-served by reading and weighing the advice of scholars whose research and teaching responsibilities have centered on the music of particular ethnic-cultural groups and who have taught as well the broad spread of musical cultures in undergraduate survey courses. Committee members suggested issues, further refined the outline, and recommended names of scholars "with an ear to education" who could be interviewed, and whose interviews might be published in the widely read *Music Educators Journal* (*MEJ*). A proposal for the series was approved by the board of the Society for Ethnomusicology and by MENC officers and editorial staff.[9]

Eight ethnomusicologists were invited to participate in the project. They represent older and younger generations of scholars (several of whom are also culture-bearers, i.e., persons whose personal/family culture is the same as that of their scholarly expertise). All are acquainted with the efforts of music educators to achieve a multicultural and global curriculum and all have been involved to some extent in these efforts—as guest teachers, "resource ethnomusicologists," members of educational panels, and/or authors of educational materials.

Letters describing the intent and procedures of the series were sent to the ethnomusicologists, along with nineteen questions and an audiotape for their responses. Issues of musical authenticity, acculturation, traditional and contemporary "popular" styles, and transmission (teaching and learning) were raised regarding the culture of their expertise, along with general concerns on ways in which musical cultures of the world could be best presented to elementary and secondary school students. Within the course of a year, tapes were returned and then transcribed, and queries and clarifications were conducted by phone, letter, and electronic mail. Guided by the remarks of the ethnomusicologists, I designed two lessons for each musical culture in order to present material deemed representative and "authentic" to the culture as well as to suggest models for school use. The series then unfolded over a 14-month period in the bimonthly *MEJ* and was labeled an "in-depth series," with "Music in Cultural Context" as the actual series title.

The "Music in Cultural Context" Collection

The collection of interview articles provides some answers to questions often asked by educators intent upon teaching the musics of a variety of world cultures to their students: What *is* world music? Which music should be highlighted in a study of Navajo culture? What styles best represent Chinese music? What music do young Iranians listen to? Is there a children's music within Nigeria? What does music mean to a group of people? What should we know about performance styles? How can we pay tribute not only to the music but to its traditional means of transmission? Is there a difference between "authentic" and "traditional" music? Are there contextual issues and cultural sensitivities to consider when teaching a designated musical style? The collection is unique in that those interviewed are principal scholars of the music they describe and are able to articulate their views on how such music can be infused within K–12 curricular structures.

Readers may find the collection useful in a number of ways: (1) as a launch to discussion (at professional meetings, on task forces and commissions, in undergraduate and graduate methods and foundations courses) of cross-cultural comparisons of music and pedagogy and of the issues of multiculturalism in music education; (2) as the basis of a discussion and demonstration of the various National Standards that pay tribute to musical diversity, with particular emphasis to content standard 9; (3) as source material for developing lessons for children, particularly since some of the lesson content has not been published elsewhere but is from my own or other ethnomusicological fieldwork; (4) as source material for developing lessons for students in secondary school and instrumental settings, demonstrating that world music is relevant not only to students of general music classes but also to members of choirs, bands, orchestras, stringed groups, and non-traditional ensembles (e.g., percussion ensembles); and (5) as evidence to present to colleagues and administrators of the significant role that music plays in a variety of cultures and of music's many functions as a human phenomenon.

Indeed, the collection is unique in that it provides a forum for discussing the challenges of attaining knowledge of musical cultures distant from one's own and the approaches educators might take in teaching a particular musical culture to students. The collection is more than the *MEJ* series in that it presents under one cover the similarities and contradictions of ideas about musical cultures and their place in the curriculum. The postlude presents a summary of the issues raised within the interviews and provides a venue for reflecting upon the responses of the ethnomusicologists—both patterns of ideas that emerged and the conflicting but thoughtful positions taken by some regarding the teaching of music in its global and multicultural manifestations.

Notes

1. For distinctions between the two practices, see Patricia Shehan Campbell, "Music Instruction: Marked and Moulded by Multiculturalism," *American Music Teacher* 42, no. 6 (1993): 14–17; 67–69.
2. James A. Banks, "Multicultural Education: Historical Development, Dimensions, and Practice," in James A. Banks and Cheryl A. McGee Banks, eds., *Handbook of Research on Multicultural Education* (New York: Macmillan, 1995): 3–24.
3. James A. Banks, "Multicultural Education: Its Effects on Students' Ethnic and Gender Role Attitudes," in J. P. Shaver, ed., *Handbook of Research on Social Studies Teaching and Learning* (New York: Macmillan, 1991): 459–469.
4. John U. Ogbu, "Overcoming Racial Barriers to Equal Access," in J. I. Goodlad and P. Keating, eds., *Access to Knowledge: An Agenda for Our Nation's Schools* (New York: McGraw-Hill, 1990): 59–89.
5. Charles Sykes and Kenneth L. Billingsley, "Multicultural Mafia," *Heterodoxy* 1, no. 5 (1992): 1, 4–6.
6. Arthur M. Schlesinger, Jr., *The Disuniting of America* (New York: Norton, 1992).
7. School orchestras, and occasionally choirs, are the most likely venues for teaching the "canon" featured in collegiate programs; listening lessons and transcriptions for band are also means for the transmission of some of these works. But due partly to the fact that beginning singers and instrumentalists do not yet possess the considerable skills necessary to perform masterworks of European high-art culture, a "school music" repertoire exists that is widely embraced by teachers of students at all levels.
8. See Terese Volk, "The History and Development of Multicultural Music Education as Evidenced in the *Music Educators Journal*, 1967–1992," *Journal of Research in Music Education* 41, no. 2 (1993): 137–156. See also Patricia Shehan Campbell, "Musica Exotica, Multiculturalism, and School Music," *Quarterly Journal of Music Teaching and Learning* 5, no. 2 (summer 1994): 65–75.
9. Betty Atterbury, then chair of the *Music Educators Journal's* editorial committee, and then MENC President-Elect Will Schmid were key players in the realization of this publication project, along with Michael Blakeslee, publications manager at the time.

MUSIC IN CULTURAL CONTEXT

DAVID P. MCALLESTER ON NAVAJO MUSIC

As part of the "Music in Cultural Context" series, this interview with David P. McAllester focuses on the music of the Navajo nation.

BY PATRICIA SHEHAN CAMPBELL

Music teachers are increasingly interested in opening their classrooms and rehearsal rooms to music that originates from outside the Western European art tradition. This interest shows up in the pages of MENC journals, in the programming for MENC conferences, and in the National Standards, which refer to study of music "representing diverse genres and cultures."

The interest stems, in part, from mandates imposed on teachers by school districts, principals, and parents, as well as by the perceived needs of the communities or neighborhoods in which they are located. But the interest brings with it a series of questions: How does one maintain musical integrity when so many new musical traditions are begging for representation? What is the authentic repertoire of a given musical culture? What should be the context in which one teaches the music of a culture? In what ways can teachers come into the music of a given tradition? Are there resources that are more valid than others for use in the classroom?

Ethnomusicology—the study of music in culture, or music as culture—can help teachers come to grips with these questions. Through this series of articles, some of the foremost scholars in that field offer their insights into the challenges of teaching world musics in the multicultural classrooms of today.

David P. McAllester, born in Everett, Massachusetts, in 1916, began his fascination with Native-American music and culture as a child. In his writings, he has recalled: "I had built my first tipi when I was eight, and I was reading ethnographies in my early teens." Today, after a lifetime of study, he is one of the foremost scholars on Native-American music and culture. As an anthropologist and ethnomusicologist, he studies music as ethnology and a way of seeing into the psychology,

Patricia Shehan Campbell is professor in the School of Music at the University of Washington in Seattle and chair of the Society for Ethnomusicology's Education Committee.

religion, and philosophy of a group of people.

McAllester's field research emphasizes music, religious literature, and ceremonialism in Navajo contexts and also in the musical cultures of the Hopis, Penobscots, Passamaquoddies, Apaches, Zunis, Comanches, Lagunas, and Menominees. Since 1981, he has undertaken archival research on the history of the Mahicans, a Native-American group who used to live in the Hudson River region.

McAllester began teaching at Wesleyan University in Middletown, Connecticut, in 1947, following his schooling at Harvard (B.A., 1938) and Columbia (Ph.D., 1949) universities. During his thirty-nine years of tenure at

Wesleyan, he founded the anthropology department and the ethnomusicology program, and was supportive and even became a symbol of broader views of music for purposes of world understanding. One of the four founders of the Society for Ethnomusicology in 1952, he served as editor of the society's journal, *Ethnomusicology*, from 1959 to 1962 and as the society's president from 1965 to 1966.

McAllester's extensive fieldwork throughout the Southwest includes study of peyote music and linguistics among the Comanches and music and ritual of the Navajo Enemyway ceremony. This work was documented in *Peyote Music* (1949) and *Enemy Way Music* (1954). Other publications followed: *Navajo Blessingway Singer* (1978, with Charlotte J. Frisbie), *Hogans, Navajo Houses, and House Songs* (1980, with Susan W. McAllester), *Worlds of Music* (1983, with Jeff Todd Titon and others), and *Becoming Human through Music* (1984).

McAllester's history of activity as an educator runs long and deep. Since the 1960s, he has lectured widely on Indian music and life before teachers' groups and students in elementary and secondary schools. He has prepared recordings for school teachers and students and published ethnomusicological articles in the *Music Educators Journal, Keyboard, Jr.,* and *Young Keyboard, Jr.* His legendary presentation at the Tanglewood Symposium in 1968, documented in his essay "The Substance of Things Hoped For," and his contributions to MENC meetings and publications helped to set the course for the inclusion of world musics in the schools. In 1984, McAllester directed the MENC-sponsored Wesleyan Symposium, an assembly of ethnomusicologists, anthropologists, and music educators who focused on the process of music transmission in other cultures. He was featured as a principal presenter at the 1990 MENC-sponsored Symposium on Multicultural Approaches to Music Education and is featured in the MENC videotape *Teaching the Music of the American Indian*, which resulted from the symposium. With so many professional accomplishments and contributions behind him, he still pursues two dominant themes in his life: nature through hiking, camping, canoeing, and natural history projects, and the music and culture of Native Americans.

Here are McAllester's answers to questions about music and culture.

When and where should world musics be taught?

Whenever possible and wherever possible. I believe that music, like every other kind of information from various cultures, helps in world understanding and, therefore, it ought to be studied as much as possible. It's better to learn

David P. McAllester

anything about other cultures, any little bit of information—a "smattering"—than nothing at all. Culture is contagious, and we learn smatterings or much more, depending on the opportunities presented to us.

Should students first learn something of Western art music, and then move on to others?

Many students never have the opportunity to learn about Western art music, even in our own culture, but instead are brought up almost entirely on popular music. I think that's all right, but I think that they should learn about as many musics as they can, including our Western art music. Yet, depending on the circles one moves in and on what one wants out of life, I don't think that Western European art music is a necessity or something that we feel we should have to teach in our school system to everybody regardless. It is only one music of many.

What channels can you recommend for teachers' pursuit of greater musical

and cultural competence in styles removed from their training and experience?

The channels I'd recommend are the recordings and the writings. *Ethnomusicology,* the journal of the Society for Ethnomusicology, would give one a start. Also, the offerings of the many different presses that feature world music are beginning to appear. World Music/West Music strikes me as one of the most comprehensive general organizations that publish multicultural materials for school use. [The address is 1208 Fifth Street, PO Box 5521, Coralville, IA 52241.]

What is the musical culture of your own expertise?

My own area of expertise is Native-American music, particularly Navajo music. Navajos live in the American Southwest; their reservation is in part of New Mexico, part of Arizona, and part of Utah. It's about twice the size of Massachusetts, 25,000 square miles—our largest reservation. The Navajos are shown on any map of Indian country (figure 1).

What is the incidence of this musical culture in the U.S.?

Representation of this musical culture in the U.S. is largely lacking, except in radio programs in the Southwest. The reason why the music is not more widely heard is that the language is difficult. The music generally just hasn't received the publicity some musics receive either. Certain popular songs in the traditional Navajo culture are quite widely heard among the Navajos, but not elsewhere.

There is a Navajo flute player who is heard all over the world: R. Carlos Nakai [Nah-KAH-ee]. He's a Navajo, but he plays a Plains-Indian flute and creates new-age music on it. He's extremely popular among the Navajos and the general public here and abroad. But the music that the Navajos think of as "old-time Navajo music" is only heard on the Navajo reservation and on certain radio programs in the Southwest.

Figure 1. Selected Native-American peoples in the U.S.

Note. Map developed from various sources, including *Harvard Encyclopedia of American Ethnic Groups* and works by David P. McAllester.

What is the meaning and function of music to the Navajos? How is it connected to life and other artistic expressions?

The meaning of the music is multiple. Most of it, in one way or another, has to do with Navajo ceremonial life. It may be popular music for dancing in ceremonies, and that dancing may occur outside of ceremonies—even before the non-Navajo public at fairs, rodeos, and other kinds of gatherings that attract non-Navajos. But in the ceremonial context, its principal use is to bring the listeners and the performers into harmony with the universe. This includes curing the sick, the depressed, or the uneasy.

Navajo ceremonial music is largely curative, but some of it is prophylactic in that it puts you in a harmonious relationship before you get sick or before you get out of that relationship. It's a restorative music, intended to restore harmony that's been lost or ensure harmony before it's lost—harmony with the community, with nature, with the deities.

Navajo music is connected to dance. It's connected to sand paintings and to weaving. There are songs for almost everything in Navajo culture, and there are new songs that go with aspects of modern Navajo culture as well.

Within the musical culture of the Navajo, what is the single "most representative" music?

If there's any single "most representative" music, it is the popular music of the traditional culture known as squaw dance songs or Enemyway dance songs. There are hundreds of these, and they're heard very widely, whereas some of the other ceremonial music is sacred and secret and not widely heard.

This music is much the same as it was several generations ago. A century ago, the popular music of the ceremonies was probably different—we don't really know how. But as it evolves, it adds more English words, and many of the songs deal with contemporary situations like meeting attractive girls in Japan during World War II, auto-

mobiles, radio programs, and motels. Many of these things are appearing with increasing frequency in squaw dance songs.

What forms of children's songs appear within Navajo culture?

There's no music specifically for children in traditional Navajo culture. Children just pick up songs that they've heard from the adults and sing parts of them. They don't merely listen; they'll join in, and they'll sing when they're by themselves. There is, however, a certain shyness that people who don't know songs show; children don't like to be heard trying to sing them unless they do know them. What they learn in school includes Western children's songs and, increasingly now, squaw dance songs and songs that are made up for them by their teachers. Otherwise, they're learning country-western, gospel, and rock and roll. Some young people have been making up new songs based on country-western models, combining them with more traditional Navajo models.

What sources can you recommend for exploring Navajo music with young people?

I'd say that one of the best sources for Native-Amcrican and Navajo music is Canyon Records [4143 N. 16 St., Phoenix, AZ, 85016]. There is also a good discography in the MENC proceedings of the Symposium on Multicultural Approaches to Music Education [*Teaching Music with a Multicultural Approach* (MENC, 1991)]. As for instruments, Navajos use only drums and rattles in their traditional music.

■ ■ ■ ■ ■ ■

There are songs for almost everything in Navajo culture.

■ ■ ■ ■ ■ ■

What introductory experiences in Navajo music can you suggest?

Start with any one of the R. Carlos Nakai recordings, published by Canyon Records. Even though he's playing a Plains-Indian flute and making up his own new-age music, it's still very Navajo in that he celebrates *places*. The word "hózhǫ́ǫ́," which means "the place is beautiful" and "the place is in harmony," is the basic concept in Navajo philosophy. Nakai celebrates the Southwest and places all over the world in his music. And that's very Navajo. If he inspires an interest in the Navajos, then a teacher might present other types of Navajo music. But Nakai's flute music is a beautiful, mellow sound, and I think it does a lot to challenge the interest of anyone.

What Navajo music could teachers use in classrooms?

There are some squaw dance songs that can be sung. There are quite a few Hopi songs, too, many to be found in the collection by Natalie Curtis Burlin, *The Indian's Book* (New York: Dover

Publications, 1968). Another source is *Navajo Music for Classroom Enrichment* (Chinle, AZ: Navajo Curriculum Center, Rough Rock Demonstration School, 1976). This fifty-four-page book contains a number of songs, some of them made up by teachers for children and others made up by children in the classroom. Some are nursery songs, humorous songs, songs with morals, Yeibichai songs from the Nightway ceremony, feather dance songs, or Enemyway ceremonial songs. There are Navajo and English texts, with two cassette tapes to accompany the book. If someone really wanted to work at using Navajo music, this book is available. I just found it myself on the Navajo reservation. There's nothing for bands. But for choral groups, a lot of people could sing the songs together in unison. [A source of Native-American songs, including Navajo songs, is *Moving within the Circle* by Bryan Burton, published by World Music Press, with a recording available.]

What Navajo music is better *not* performed?

For the most part, Navajo ceremonial music should not be performed by schoolchildren or, in some cases, should not even be listened to. But it's not available to be listened to anyway.

What should we know about performance styles?

Navajos traditionally sing in a somewhat more nasal voice than we do. If you had a recording, you would hear that and could imitate it.

In teaching the music of the Navajos, what should teachers know about cultural values and behaviors that may be deemed unacceptable by Navajos?

In the case of the Navajos, and Native Americans in general, I've noticed considerable touchiness about "wannabe Indians" acting like Indians in the classroom, wearing Indian costumes, and making up Indian ceremonies. There are some Indians who mind that and will say, "Everything we do is sacred and is only to be used by us." Other Indians are just amused or even glad to see anybody interested in any way. I guess the key is respect. People are often quite delighted to hear

Objectives

Students will:

■ be able to graph the rise and fall of the melody

■ be able to represent in movement the flow and energy of individual phrases

■ be able to explain the context and meaning of the piece

■ be able to play parts of the melody on recorder, flute, or other wind instruments.

Materials

■ "Origins" from *Cycles: Native American Flute Music* by R. Carlos Nakai, recorded on Canyon CR-614 (volume 2)

■ paper and pencil; blackboard

■ recorder, flute, or other wind instruments

■ timpani, or other tuned drums, or cello or bass

Procedures

1. Provide information on the song. "Origins" is part of an eight-part musical work, *Cycles*, by R. Carlos Nakai. The work was created for the multimedia presentation "Our Voices, Our Land," presented at the Heard Museum in Phoenix, Arizona. Nakai features Native-American flute and synthesizer in *Cycles,* intending to portray sound experiences that he has "felt" while on the vast, open expanses of the Southwest and Northern Plains. He describes his inspiration for "Origins" in this way: "My clan, Naashteezhi dine-e Taachiinii, allows me to be one of the people." Thus, the piece is his musical reflection on his

"Origins" Lesson Plan
by Patricia Shehan Campbell

participation as part of an extended family, a clan, of the Navajo people.

2. Play the recording of "Origins." Ask students to listen to the rise and fall of the flute melody. In another listening, ask them to "paint" or "draw" the rising and falling lines in the air.

3. As the students listen again to the recording, ask them to begin moving at the start of each melodic phrase and to stop at the end of the phrase. Encourage them to move first with hands and arms only (in place), then to move with their feet, and then to involve the body more fully—turning, twisting, and stretching. When the movement begins to flow, challenge students to change direction with each new melodic phrase they hear.

4. Ask students to use paper and pencil or the blackboard to draw the rise and fall of each melodic line. More advanced students might be challenged to notate what they hear.

5. Provide students with some of the melodic phrases, or frameworks, for "Origins"—see the music excerpts. Have the students play these phrases on recorder, flute, or other wind instruments. When these phrases are "under the fingers," suggest that the students take turns in small or large groups, improvising and extending these phrases. Timpani, or other tuned drums, or cello or bass can provide the grounding pitch.

6. Discuss the duality of honoring traditional features of a musical culture while developing new personal expressions, as in Nakai's work that blends traditional flute with synthesizer.

Melodic phrase samplings from "Origins."

their songs sung by somebody outside the culture and to know that somebody outside the culture is even interested. In the case of Navajo songs, when I sing them to Navajos, they are amazed that some outsider sings them and often ascribe greater expertise to me than I really have.

■ ■ ■ ■ ■ ■

Any culture is constantly in flux, with new ideas coming into vogue.

■ ■ ■ ■ ■ ■

One answer to this important issue might be that it's up to those groups themselves to make known to cultures with which they come in contact what aspects of their culture they do not want imitated—just as, I think, we Western Europeans make it clearly understood that we don't want our church music imitated in any disrespectful way. If you teach in a school system in Navajo country and want to introduce Navajo music to the children, the thing would be to consult with the children and, particularly, their parents. Ask them whether they have any objections to this or that kind of music being used in the school or whether they have suggestions as to what would be the kind of music you might teach.

What contextual features should be kept in mind when teaching Navajo music?

I was invited to go to the Red Rock High School on the Navajo reservation to consult with their school board about using Navajo music in their curriculum. And we, a group of teachers and I, ended up going and talking to a nearby ceremonial practitioner, or medicine man. He named certain types of music. He said that he thought squaw dance music and peyote music would be all right to use in

the classroom, but "why do it?" He said that "it would be out of context." He didn't see any reason for singing these songs out of their natural setting. But he didn't see any harm in it, either.

When I thought about that, I began to realize that much of our education is out of context. Much of what we teach is *as if* you were an engineer or *as if* you were a mathematician. This is the foundation of our educational philosophy. So, if Navajos want their children to go to that kind of school, then they should expect this kind of approach. This medicine man was not objecting. He was just curious about what use these songs would be in the school context. He wanted to know how we could answer that question with our interest in multiple-cultural understanding.

What else can you tell us that would increase our sensitivity to Navajo people, their music, and their cultural values?

I recently happened in on a song-and-dance session in a school gymnasium in an elementary school in the middle of the Navajo reservation. The people who were performing there were dressed in Navajo costumes—they were Navajos. They were dressed in old-style costumes, and they'd paid something to enter and compete in certain classes of dancing and singing in order to win prizes. Other people were paying admission to attend the event, as the competition was a benefit to raise money for the school. There were refreshments, and the event was much like a neighborhood social with people singing and dancing Navajo songs and dances.

But that kind of event, I heard, was controversial. There were some elders, traditional Navajos, who were objecting and saying that the songs and dances were out of context and, therefore, shouldn't be done. But these performing groups are springing up all over the reservation, and the old people are beginning to accept them.

So, one point to be made is that no generalization you can make about a culture or situation is set in concrete. Any culture is constantly in flux, with new ideas coming into vogue. There are always new ways of doing things and new ways for people to make music that are meaningful to them at a given time and place. ■

Objectives

Students will:

- be able to keep the pulse of the song while listening to it
- be able to sing a Navajo children's song
- be able to explain the song's cultural meaning
- be able to perform a circle dance while singing.

Materials

- "Shanile" music (see the trancription—the song has been transposed into a comfortable singing key for the children)
- drum

Procedures

1. Provide information on the song. "Shanile" is a children's song first recorded in 1956 in Flagstaff, Arizona. The singers were Margaret Edaaki, a Winnebago woman, and her husband, War Bow, a Zuni man. The couple had often performed at Indian shows and had taught in Indian schools.

2. Discuss Navajo traditional life as it existed forty years ago, when children were given new "going-to-school" shoes by their parents for beginning their studies in September, after having worn out their old shoes while at play all summer long. The new shoes were often Sears Roebuck shoes, obtained at a trading post. Discuss the existence of the practice today, in various communities and cultures, when children dress in ways appropriate for the activities of play, school, worship, or parties.

3. While you sing the song, ask the students to find the pulse and pat, tap,

"Shanile" Lesson Plan
by Patricia Shehan Campbell

or conduct it. The singing can be done without seeing notation, as the song is traditionally transmitted orally. Students should be directed to join in singing the song when they feel ready.

4. Give the translation of the song:

> You gave them to me!
> You gave them to me!
> You gave them to me!
> My shoes, you gave them to me!
> With those (shoes), I went
>   (to school), he, ne, ya!

> With those shoes I went,
> With those shoes I went,
> With those shoes I went.
> My shoes, you gave them to me.
> With those (shoes), I went
>   (to school), he, ne, ya!

5. Sing the song with appropriate stresses on the accented syllables, while continuing to keep the pulse. Play the pulse on the drum. Note that a squaw dance is the only Navajo song accompanied by drum, a small water drum made of a clay pot with a buckskin cover and tuned by adjusting the level of water in the pot.

6. Perform a round dance while singing "Shanile." Form a circle facing inward, made up of two sides representing the home camp and the "enemy" camp. Half the circle sings while everyone steps in one direction, and then the song is repeated, this time sung by the other half while everyone steps in the opposite direction. The foot movement is sideways, moving clockwise (to the left). The left foot begins, followed by the right foot, in this repeated pattern:

The song can be repeated many times, reversing the direction of the dance movements and alternating between home camp and enemy camp each time the song is sung.

"Shanile," recorded and transcribed by David P. McAllester, © 1956. Used by permission.

MUSIC IN CULTURAL CONTEXT

TERRY E. MILLER ON THAI MUSIC

As part of the "Music in Cultural Context" series, this interview with Terry E. Miller focuses on music of Thailand and, more generally, Southeast Asia.

BY PATRICIA SHEHAN CAMPBELL

Terry E. Miller was born in Dover, Ohio, a "twin city" of New Philadelphia on the Tuscarawas River, in 1945. As a child, he enjoyed looking at maps and collecting stamps, so that he knew "where things were" in the world. He studied piano and harpsichord at the College of Wooster, where he received his bachelor's degree in music. He continued his musical studies at Indiana University and became interested in the Southern shape-note tradition and oral tradition hymnody.

Then, major changes were in store for him. As he tells it, "I got drafted into the U.S. Army and was sent to Southeast Asia in 1969. The first non-Western music that I experienced 'live' was Vietnamese in Vietnam. I was able to see theater performances in Saigon, to visit the national conservatory, and to collect Vietnamese recordings and musical instruments. After two years back in the U.S., I returned to Southeast Asia to write my doctoral thesis on kaen [a free-reed mouth organ] and mawlum [singing style]

Patricia Shehan Campbell is professor in the School of Music at the University of Washington in Seattle and chair of the Society for Ethnomusicology's Education Committee.

Terry E. Miller

music of northeast Thailand."

Miller completed his doctorate at Indiana University. He began teaching at Kent State University in 1975, where he currently is a professor of ethnomusicology. During his tenure there, he has established the ethnomusicology program's Thai and Chinese performing ensembles and has continued to be the only university teacher of Lao kaen in the U.S. He is

cofounder of the Center for the Study of World Musics and works closely not only with ethnomusicology students but also with music educators interested in developing a world perspective on music and its instruction.

After fourteen years, Miller returned to Thailand in 1988, and has done so three times since then. He was in Laos in 1973, 1974, and 1991, and in Cambodia in 1988. More than twenty years passed between his service in Vietnam and his recent research visits in 1991, 1993, and 1994, during which he documented musical performances from the Mekong Delta all the way north to Hanoi. His publications include two books, *Traditional Music of the Lao* (Greenwood Press, 1985) and *American Folk Music: An Annotated Bibliography* (Greenwood Press, 1986). His recordings include the music of Laos, the Chinese sheng (mouth organ), and Vietnamese music in the U.S. While he is keen to write a book on lined-out hymnody, based on fieldwork in the U.S., Scotland, Jamaica, Trinidad, and St. Vincent, it is his continued research on the music of Southeast Asians that has brought others the potential for understanding some of the newest Americans, their musical interests, and their homeland cultures.

12   MUSIC IN CULTURAL CONTEXT

Here are Miller's responses to questions about music of Thailand, Southeast Asia, and the world at large.

Should the teaching of music to students begin with Western art music, and then proceed to other world traditions and genres?

It seems to me that the function of education is to open new doors for students, to offer alternatives and options to the experiences they've already had. If teachers start with Western art music as a base camp, then there is the suggestion that everything must be compared to it. Western art music then becomes the universal standard by which all other music is measured. I think we understand that music has a wider function in society than merely being an object of art to be admired; consequently, I think that if we're trying to get young people to understand how music operates within human society, we can, from the beginning, provide students with experiences in music from a variety of world cultures.

Given teachers' tight schedules, what recommendations can you offer them for the pursuit of greater musical and cultural competence in styles removed from their training and experience?

As teachers, we are faced with choices. We can't do everything, but we must decide what our priorities are. Once they are decided, we must build a base of experience and knowledge for ourselves. That's not something we can get from reading a book or taking a crash course. Competence requires that we listen, read, study videos, and, when possible, go out to the communities to experience a musical culture.

Please offer a brief geographic profile of Thailand, Laos, Vietnam, and Cambodia.

South of China and east of India, "Mainland" Southeast Asia encompasses Vietnam, Laos, Cambodia, Thailand, Myanmar (formerly Burma), and Malaysia [see figure 1]. The island countries of Southeast Asia, including Indonesia and the Philippines, lie south of the Southeast Asian mainland. Portions of the region are covered by rain forests, yet there is topographic diversity in the mountains, plains, deltas, marshes, and fertile river valleys that make up the landscape.

■ ■ ■ ■ ■

"Teachers sometimes sing traditional and popular songs with their children, or lead children in chanting mathematical principles or grammar rules."

■ ■ ■ ■ ■

The Mekong (actually "Mae nam khong"—"mae nam" means river) River has dominated the economies of people living near it. It forms the border between much of Laos and northeastern Thailand, cuts through central Cambodia, and then divides into the Nine Dragons (Cuu Long) in southern Vietnam. There it actually becomes nine broad rivers flowing to the sea and adding land by depositing silt. While Bangkok, Thailand, has become one of the Asian centers of international trade and commerce, many of Southeast Asia's inhabitants still engage in agricultural pursuits. This is "rice bowl" country, the site of the world's greatest production of rice, in a climate that is (except for mountainous regions in northern Thailand, Laos, and along the Vietnamese border) warm, humid, and affected by a wet monsoon season that runs from May to November.

Who are the people of Thailand?

The historical Tai peoples trace their origins to southern China ["Tai" refers to the linguistic/ethnic group; "Thai" refers to the people of the kingdom and nation]. They spread from southern China over a long period and probably lived among other peoples, including the Khmer of Cambodia. Tai-speaking peoples are spread today from Gueizhou through northern Vietnam, through most of Laos into Thailand and northern Myanmar. [See the Historical Sketch sidebar for a brief summary of Thailand's past.]

What is the incidence of Thai, Vietnamese, Lao, and Cambodian (Khmer) people in the U.S.?

There are about 100,000 Thai in the U.S., living for the most part in California, New York, and Illinois. Many young women married U.S. servicemen during the Vietnam War; others are professionals, including doctors and nurses.

There are more than a million Vietnamese immigrants, about 300,000 Cambodians, and at least 100,000 Lao immigrants, including the Hmong people of rural upland Laos. Many were formerly refugees, but are now well integrated into American society. In the 1970s, many refugees were brought to reception centers in California, Arkansas, Florida, and Pennsylvania, or resettled by church groups in the north central states. Today, the largest communities of Vietnamese, Cambodian, Lao, and Hmong people are found in the Los Angeles, Fresno, Seattle, and Boston areas, and in several Gulf Coast communities (especially in Texas).

Your expertise focuses on which musical cultures?

My areas of expertise include the American shape-note singing school; lined-out hymnody in Appalachia, the Scottish Hebrides, Jamaica, Trinidad, and St. Vincent; and musical cultures of Southeast Asia, principally Thailand, Laos, Vietnam, and, lastly, Cambodia.

What music do people in Thailand prefer? What music represents the Thai people?

The greatest percentage of Thai

people spend their time and money on various kinds of popular music. In rural areas, people still perform and listen to folk or village music, sometimes in modernized forms. But in central Thailand, and certainly in Bangkok, young people listen to American-derived rock music. For older people, Phleng Luk Tung, a popular music derived from regional musical styles (particularly northeastern Thailand), holds great appeal.

It's interesting that Thai people abroad use Thai classical music to represent their culture, because it was never intended to be the music of the people. The classical music of the royal courts was originally the elite music of the aristocracy. It remains the music of a small but sophisticated group of people, but is also taught in colleges and in some schools. This classical music is completely integrated into dance and theater forms, and is rarely performed without one or the other. Throughout Southeast Asia, musical research has centered on traditions of the royal courts, even when folk and pop/rock styles are far more representative of the interests of the people.

What are the instruments of Thai classical music?

There are several types of ensembles historically associated with the royal courts of Thailand (as well as Cambodia and Laos), including the pi phat and mahori. Pi phat music is played on higher- and lower-pitched wooden xylophones (called ranat), circles of knobbed kettle gongs (called kong wong), the pi quadruple-reed oboe, drums, and other percussion instruments. Instruments of the mahori ensemble include fiddles, zither, flute, xylophones, gong circles, and drums. Carl Orff became acquainted with the Thai ranat, and eventually modeled his xylophones on this instrument.

What music do Thai children learn?

Music is not a required subject for study in the Thai schools. Teachers sometimes sing traditional and popular songs with their children, or lead children in chanting mathematical principles or grammar rules. Outside of school, Thai children participate in religious ceremonies and are exposed to the chants and songs associated with worship.

There are a few exceptional schools where music is deemed important for study. At a secondary school in a village southeast of Bangkok, a large building was built on the school grounds just for music. In the early morning, children from eight to seventeen years of age learn the instruments and repertoire of Thai classical music in the traditional way, by observing and imitating the performance of their teachers. These students even practice the custom of "wai kru," paying homage to their music teachers. At another school in Bangkok, students use computer programs, following graphics and bouncing balls to learn traditional instruments.

What sources can you recommend for exploring Thai (and Southeast

Figure 1. Southeast Asia, Mainland

Asian) music with young people?

There's little available on Thai music outside of Thailand. Two recordings I'd recommend are *The Flower of Isan* [Globestyle CD OR BD051] and *Thailand: Music of the Northeast* [Lyrichord LLST 7357]. Both feature the traditional music of northeastern Thailand, including the free-reed mouth organ (kaen). Ethnic Folkways produced *Music of Thailand* [Ethnic Folkways FE 4463] in the 1960s, on which there are several classical Thai pieces. Court music from Cambodia and Laos is presented on *Musiques de l'Asie Traditionnelle*, volumes 1 and 2 [Playasound PS 33501 (Cambodia) and PS 33502 (Laos)]. The *JVC Anthology of Music of the World's People* [published by the Japan Video Corporation] includes several segments on classical and folk music from Thailand, Cambodia, and Vietnam, but there are problems with each of them (the Vietnamese examples are a serious problem), including the erroneous presentation of particular genres and instruments as representative of a culture. [The Resources sidebar provides additional resources—books and recordings—for learning about the music of Southeast Asia.]

What suggestions do you have for teachers and their students who wish to learn (or learn about) Thai music?

If you can't go to Southeast Asia, you can go to the communities of Southeast Asians in the U.S. There are summer festivals, religious celebrations, New Year's parties, and other events sponsored by Thai, Vietnamese, Cambodian, Lao, and Hmong groups at their temples and community centers. This past summer, the Smithsonian Institution featured Thailand at its Folklife Festival in Washington, D.C. State and local arts groups and folklore agencies occasionally sponsor similar events and can serve as helpful contacts for communities of southeast Asians.

What experiences in Thai music could a teacher offer to students?

There are certainly listening experiences that can be designed and traditional songs that can be sung. There is

no material available for orchestra or band. Traditional melodies can be played on Orff xylophones, particularly if the bars are "doctored up" with modeling clay to match the Thai tuning system of seven equidistant pitches within the octave.

■ ■ ■ ■ ■

"Outside of school, Thai children participate in religious ceremonies and are exposed to the chants and songs associated with worship."

■ ■ ■ ■ ■

Particularly important to an understanding of Thai music is the matter of embedding it within the culture. What's the purpose of playing Thai melodies on specially tuned xylophones if students don't know where

Thailand is or *what* it is? They need to have a sense of the geography and history of Thailand. They need to know something of the people who make the music. How can you make all this real? Through videotapes and, when possible, through Thai visitors to the classroom.

What should we know about transmission styles within Thailand (and Southeast Asia)?

We would learn a lot about teaching, and about a culture, by observing how music is transmitted. As in most of the world, music in Thailand and throughout Southeast Asia is learned by rote. New students sit in on rehearsals of an ensemble and observe the more experienced musicians. They are then given a simple rhythm instrument to play. Gradually, as they get used to the sound, they're given greater responsibilities and are assigned new instruments to play. The rote system is very time-intensive, but it's also very thorough—you never forget the music.

In teaching the music of Southeast Asians, what should teachers know about the values that these people now living in the U.S. place upon their music?

Most of the Thai who live in America are affluent, Americanized, and would not expect Thai music to be taught in the schools. I've also found that the children of refugees (the Vietnamese, Cambodian, Lao, and

Hmong), that is, the generation born in the U.S., seldom have a strong interest in or knowledge of their home country. While Vietnamese folk songs are tuneful and can be taught and even arranged for instruments, teachers would be hard-pressed to make sense of Hmong music unless they knew the Hmong language. Hmong music is language-based poetry declamation.

A word of warning: Steer clear of national anthems. They're almost never typical of the country, and some countries change anthems as frequently as they change governments. Also, any materials recently arriving from Vietnam, Cambodia, and Laos may present a political problem to immigrants, who may not recognize the present governments. When in doubt, ask.

What else can you tell us that would be helpful to think about when teaching the music of Southeast Asia and, even more generally, when considering world music education?

In the cases of Thailand and Cambodia, it can't hurt to convey to students the relationship between teachers and students, and the manner in which teaching is still a highly regarded profession of honor. American students should be made aware of the reverence and ritual bestowed upon teachers by their students in much of Southeast Asia; the current teacher is the last and most recent teacher of a long sacred line of past teachers. Certain rules of etiquette are as important to the musical culture as the music itself. Students should be made aware of such rules as "Don't touch people on the head," "Don't point with your feet," and "Step around rather than over musical instruments."

More generally, it seems important for teachers to consider the option of teaching fewer musical cultures, but teaching them in greater depth than a broad survey allows. Teachers might make a more significant impact on their students' development if they concentrated on learning a few musical traditions well and teaching them. Of course, learning is a lifelong process, and teachers with curiosity will press for all the information that they can bring to their students. ∎

▬ *Resources for Southeast Asian Music* ▬

Thailand

The Flower of Isan. Globestyle CD OR BD051.

Morton, David. "The Music of Thailand," in Elizabeth May, ed., *Music of Many Cultures,* 63–81. Los Angeles: University of California Press, 1982.

Music of Thailand. Ethnic Folkways FE 4463.

Thailand: Music of the Northeast. Lyrichord LLST 7357.

Yupho, Dhanit. *The Custom and Rite of Paying Homage to Teachers.* Bangkok: The Fine Arts Department, 1974.

Cambodia

Cambodia, Musical Atlas. EMI C-064-17841.

Music of Cambodia. World Music Institute WMI-007.

Musiques de l'Asie Traditionnelle volume 1. Playasound PS 33501.

Royal Music of Cambodia. Phillips 6586 002.

Sam, Sam-Ang, and Patricia Shehan Campbell. *Silent Temples, Songful Hearts: Traditional Music of Cambodia.* Danbury, CT: World Music Press, 1992.

Laos (Lao and Hmong)

De Roin, Nancy. *Jataka Tales.* New York: Dell Yearling, 1975.

Laos. Bärenreiter 30 L2001.

Miller, Terry E. *The Traditional Music of the Lao: Kaen Playing and Mawlum Singing in Northeast Thailand.* Westport, CT: Greenwood Press, 1985.

Musiques de l'Asie Traditionnelle, volume 2. Playasound PS 33502.

Sounds of the World: Music of Southeast Asia. Reston, VA: Music Educators National Conference, 1986. (Three tapes on Lao, Hmong, and Vietnamese music, with a study guide written by Patricia K. Shehan)

Vietnam

Eternal Voices: Traditional Vietnamese Music of the U.S. New Alliance NAR 053.

Instrumental Music of Vietnam: Dan Tranh. World Music Enterprises WME 1007.

Music of Vietnam. Lyrichord LLST 7337.

Nguyen, Phong Thuyet, and Patricia Shehan Campbell. *From Rice Paddies and Temple Yards: Traditional Music of Vietnam.* Danbury, CT: World Music Press, 1990.

Pham, Duy. *Musics of Vietnam.* Carbondale, IL: Southern Illinois University Press, 1975.

"Mon Son Pha" Lesson Plan

by Patricia Shehan Campbell

Objectives

Students will:

- be able to tap a steady pulse while listening to the teacher's recitation of a Thai folk chant

- be able to approximate the durations and pitch inflections of Thai language

- be able to explain the meaning and context of the chant

- be able to play the game that corresponds to the chant

- be able to graph the rising, falling, and flat tones of Thai language

Materials

- the notated chant (for the teacher's use only, since it should be transmitted orally)

- a scarf

- paper and pencil, blackboard

- recorders

Procedures

1. Provide information on the chant. "Mon Son Pha" is Thai for "Mon Hiding the Cloth." The Mon are a minority group living in western Thailand, near the Myanmar border. At Songkran (Thai New Year), children and adults play a game with a twisted cloth while chanting the rhyme rhythmically. The rhyme is translated: "I am hiding a piece of cloth. The cloth is behind my back. Leave it here? Leave it there? I will tap you on the back."

2. Ask students to keep a steady pulse while you chant the words. Memorize the chant so that it can be delivered orally. Pay special attention to a crisp rhythmic delivery and to the rising, falling, and flat tones indicated in the notation. Falling tones drop approximately a third to a fourth (interval).

3. Teach the chant, shown below, either in small segments or by the immersion process, in which students listen repeatedly and then gradually join in the chant when they feel ready to do so. Remind them to be sensitive to the rise and fall of Thai tonal language.

4. When students can chant the verse while patting the pulse, teach them the game. Twist a long scarf and then double it, bringing the two ends together. Have the students form a circle while they pat or clap the pulse and chant the verse repeatedly. A designated scarf-hider, holding the scarf, walks on the outside of the circle. At any point, he or she may tap the back of another student, who then chases the scarf-hider around the circle. The scarf-hider finds safety in the spot vacated by the "tapped student," who then gets the scarf and becomes the next scarf-hider (unless the tapped student managed to outrun the original scarf-hider and get back to the vacated spot first).

5. Challenge students to graph the rising, falling, and flat tones of the Thai language. They can use paper and pencil to do this or go to the blackboard.

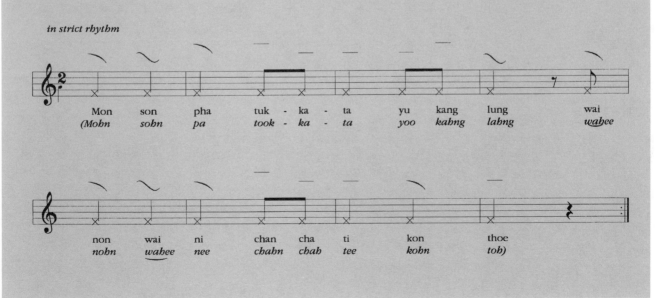

"Lai sootsanaen" Lesson Plan

by Patricia Shehan Campbell

Objectives

Students will:

- be able to keep a quick and steady pulse while listening to a musical selection for xylophones from northeastern Thailand

- be able to sing the lum scale in a mode known as "lai sootsanaen" (d e g a b)

- be able to sing (and then play on xylophones) small melodic phrases based on "lai sootsanaen"

- be able to create in pairs their own "lai sootsanaen" pieces

Materials

- "Lai sootsanaen" from *Thailand: Lao Music of the Northeast* (Lyrichord LLST 7357)

- Xylophones (wooden only)

- Hard mallets (not rubber or cloth-covered)

Procedures

1. Play the recording of "lai sootsanaen," directing students to (a) identify the instruments and (b) pat a quick and steady pulse while listening. The wooden logs approximate a xylophone called "kaw-law." The excerpt on the recording features two kaw-law players providing melody and drone and imitating the sound of the free-reed mouth organ called "kaen."

2. Sing the lum pentatonic scale, in the mode known as "lai sootsanaen," which extends from d to d (d e g a b). Consider using solfège syllables (s, l, d r m).

3. Using neutral or solfège syllables, sing the melodic patterns shown below. Have the students imitate you. Pat a steady quarter-note pulse while singing.

4. Remove the F (F#) and B (Bb) bars from the xylophones. As one or several students play drone tones, lead others in playing the sung melodic patterns. Begin slowly, and then increase the speed of these patterns. Encourage the students to invent other patterns to be sung and then played by the class.

5. Assign the students, in pairs, the task of creating a "lai sootsanaen" piece with melody and quarter-note drone, as shown below, for their xylophones. These pieces can then be performed for the class.

6. Listen again to the recording of "lai sootsanaen." Ask the students to compare their musical inventions with the recorded example. They will probably be amazed and challenged by the virtuosity of the kaw-law players of northeastern Thailand.

dominant drone

BRUNO NETTL ON MUSIC OF IRAN

As part of the "Music in Cultural Context" series, this interview with Bruno Nettl focuses on music of Iran and, more generally, the Middle East.

BY PATRICIA SHEHAN CAMPBELL

Born into a musical family in the musical city of Prague in 1930, Bruno Nettl immigrated to the U.S. in 1939. His father was a noted musicologist who studied seventeenth- and eighteenth-century Austrian music, and his mother was a pianist and piano teacher. Nettl studied piano and violin from an early age, and participated as a young child in the Dalcroze eurhythmics classes his mother taught in Prague and in Princeton, New Jersey. Two events in his childhood led him to a lifelong pursuit of the study of music in culture: At the age of six, he heard one of his father's students announce that he "was going to India, where much of the music was improvised." Then, that same year, his father brought home Erich von Hornbostel's *Musiques de Oriente,* the first recorded anthology of world music from Asia—Indonesia, India, the Middle East, China, and Japan. These new musical sounds and the concept of improvisation launched Nettl's interests in the music of the world's many cultures.

Patricia Shehan Campbell is professor in the School of Music at the University of Washington in Seattle and chair of the Society for Ethnomusicology's Education Committee.

Bruno Nettl

Nettl pursued musical studies, as well as anthropology, folklore, and linguistics, at Indiana University, where he received his bachelor's, master's, and doctoral degrees in musicology. As was typical of ethnomusicological studies of the time, his first area of research examined musical styles of the American Indian. He has since done further field research with Native-American peoples, particularly

Photo courtesy of the author

the Blackfoot, and has done fieldwork in Iran and southern India.

Nettl is a visionary in the field of ethnomusicology, an important teacher and mentor to younger scholars, and probably the field's most prolific writer. He has authored, coauthored, or edited eighteen books. Among the best known are *Theory and Method in Ethnomusicology* (1964), *Folk and Traditional Music of the Western Continents* (3rd ed., 1990), *The Study of Ethnomusicology: Twenty-nine Issues and Concepts* (1983), *The Western Impact on World Music* (1985), and *Heartland Excursions: Ethnomusicological Perspectives on Schools of Music* (1994). His edited recordings include *A Persian Heritage* (Nonesuch), *A Historical Album of Blackfoot Indian Music* (Folkways), and *The Persian Radif* (Elephant & Cat). He was president of the Society for Ethnomusicology from 1969 to 1971, and earlier served as editor of the Society's journal (1961–65).

Over the years, Nettl has contributed thoughtfully to ideas regarding music teaching and transmission, and multiculturalism and world music. He presented a comparative analysis of music transmission systems at the MENC-sponsored Wesleyan Symposium in 1984, and has offered provocative world music seminars for teachers. Nettl is chair of the International Society for Music Education's Panel on Music of the World's Cultures, which recently made recommendations for introducing world musics to musical education systems in the sixty-three member-nations. Since 1964, he has taught at the University of Illinois, where he is now professor emeritus of music and anthropology.

Here are Nettl's answers to questions about music of Iran and the Middle East.

When, where, and how should world musics be taught?

In all kinds of contexts. In schools, music of the world's cultures ought to be taught as part of a music program, as both a listening and a participating activity. It should also make an appearance in the social science curriculum—geography, history, and social studies classes. It should be taught, on the one hand, as a subject that presents music as a single, world-wide phenomenon and, on the other hand, as a field in which each culture has a separate kind of musical system.

Should initial teaching/learning experiences encompass Western art music, with instruction in world music to proceed later? Or should there be equal treatment of the world's musical cultures from the start?

It may be best to start instruction with some kind of intercultural group of concepts and sounds. Students have already learned something of Western music when they arrive at school (the line between art music and other kinds of Western music, including popular music, is not all that sharp). The basic language of Western music, its functional harmony, and its four-square meters are already known by children, so that this acquired music makes for a point of departure for learning other kinds of music. I don't think that we should provide a very thorough understanding of Western art music, and then move on to other kinds of music as a secondary activity. The parity of the world's musical cultures should somehow be presented right at the beginning.

How should teachers pursue greater knowledge of the world's musical cultures?

There's no way of teaching music without "putting in time." Summer workshops and short courses are helpful. An even better approach to understanding more of the world's musics might be through a carefully structured master's degree, or some kind of systematic training in which one could commit oneself to several summers of full-time work.

■ ■ ■ ■ ■ ■

Many, if not most, tones are "bent" or are embellished with trills, glissandos, or short secondary notes.

■ ■ ■ ■ ■ ■

Independently, teachers might also utilize their summer time in order to prepare listening and study kits for their students. In the meantime, one should do what one can. In a way, some things are worth doing—even when they are not done too well—until, through further study, they can be done better.

What is the musical culture of your own expertise?

I've done field research with Northern Plains Indians, particularly the Blackfoot people of Montana, and I've done field work in Iran and southern India.

Specifically, what was the nature of your work in Iran?

I lived in the capital city of Tehran when, in the late 1960s and early 1970s, the population was about four million people. I worked with a very

small group of musicians who were devoted to classical Persian music. There were between one and two hundred professional musicians in all of Iran at that time. I also observed an even smaller group of musicians active in Middle Eastern popular music, Western popular music, and Western art music.

What is the representation of Persian classical music in the U.S.?

There is a rather large Iranian population in the U.S., but it's mostly people who have arrived since the 1960s. They reside almost entirely in large cities, particularly in Los Angeles, but also in New York and Chicago, and to a smaller extent in Seattle, Portland, and San Francisco. Persian classical music did not have much of a following in Iran, but Iranians in the U.S. have begun to build a system of classical music performances. They support these performances, participating largely to the exclusion of non-Iranians. They do not keep non-Iranians away, but assume that no one but themselves would really understand this music. They are pleasantly surprised when someone else does seem to take an interest in it.

What is the meaning of music to Iranians, in Iran and in the U.S.?

U.S. Iranians tend to identify with classical Persian music even if they don't know it well. They insist on the music's "Iranian-ness." In 1970, this music separated Iranian culture from that of other neighboring countries and cultures. But then, listening to classical Persian music was just a bit dangerous, as it demonstrated the listener as a very traditional person (too traditional, perhaps), or it suggested that the listener was a modern person who was not appropriately concerned about the Shiite Muslim clergy's proscription and disapproval of music.

Besides classical Persian music, what other musical styles are practiced in Iran?

There is the folk music of various rural groups—mostly vocal music—that is associated with the concepts and events of Islamic history and tradition. In the cities, there is the mixing of Western, traditional Persian, and other Asian elements that, in 1970, anticipated the world beat phenomenon [a phrase associated with the fusion of popular music and elements of an indigenous traditional music]. Some pieces combine Persian and European, Persian and Indian, Persian and Arabic, or Persian and Russian characteristics. The Koran is always sung, and although this is not regarded as part of the musical system in Iran, it structurally *is* music.

There is little dance music or theatre music. Music in Iran is largely something for listening to—at formal concerts, at private house concerts, on recordings, and on radio. Group participation such as choral singing is unusual. Music is largely a solo presentation, with someone performing for someone else.

Is there a single "most representative" music of Iran and Iranians?

Even though very few Iranians know classical Persian music, or participate in it as performers or listeners, most would say it represents them. The folk musics are too regional, and popular music is not very traditional. About classical Persian music, they would say, "Ah, that's the music of our nation."

How is the music of Iran today different from the music of previous generations?

There are some important elements of change during the last thirty to forty years. Western instruments, including the violin and the piano, are sometimes used to perform traditional melodies or to improvise in traditional modes. Ensemble music is more important than it used to be. Composed music, as compared to improvisation, has begun to be more important. More recently, some of the music is reverting to earlier forms and kinds of performance practice, including the removal of some of the Western elements.

Are there elements of Iran's music that are characteristic of other Middle Eastern sounds?

The Middle Eastern culture area is centered in the region of Iran, Turkey,

■ ■ ■ ■ ■ ■

Rhythm in Middle Eastern music can be equally complex, including nonmetric music and music in a variety of meters.

■ ■ ■ ■ ■ ■

and the heartland of Arabic culture—Saudi Arabia, Syria, Iraq, Lebanon, and Egypt (see figure 1). This very large area is surely quite diverse musically, but it, nevertheless, holds in common certain characteristics of musical culture and style. The music is monophonic or heterophonic, with simultaneous variations

of the melody, and there is no system of harmony to accompany the melody. Many, if not most, tones are "bent" or are embellished with trills, glissandos, or short secondary notes. The more ornamented a passage is, the better and more expressive its audience perceives it to be.

Much of the music is improvised, centered on modes called dastgāhs in Iran and maqāms in the Arabic world. These modes often consist of quarter-tones, half-tones, and whole tones (which may render some of the modes unplayable on certain fixed-key instruments like the piano). Rhythm in Middle Eastern music can be equally complex, including nonmetric music and music in a variety of meters (two, three, six, seven, and ten, for example). Middle Eastern singing can be described as throaty, nasalized, and with a tense sound. Likewise, traditional bowed lutes like the kamancha have a flat, nasal tone without vibrato, in contrast to the fuller, vibrated sound of the Western violin.

What are some of the Middle Eastern attitudes toward music?

In Middle Eastern Muslim societies, music is simultaneously feared and loved, enjoyed but viewed with

Figure 1. Iran and nearby countries

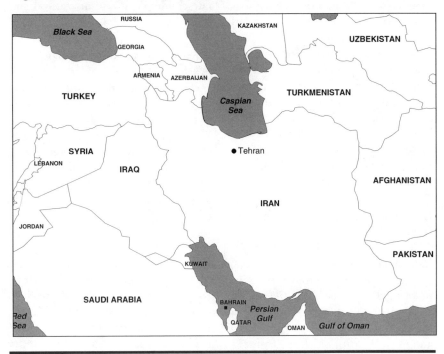

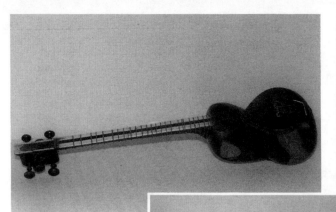

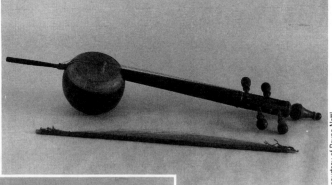

Classical Persian instruments include the tār (upper left), the kamancha (upper right), and the santur (above).

suspicion; it is subject to a kind of ambivalence. In Islamic societies, music must be kept far from the centers of religion; devout Muslims should avoid it. Instruments are to be viewed with suspicion, and dancing is to be viewed with even more suspicion.

While Iranians and Turks take their traditions of poetry and visual art and their miniatures and carpets very seriously, they cannot imagine that music deserves the same dignified treatment. But if music making was historically dangerous, the intellectual study of music was not, and there developed in Islamic society a tradition of scholarship that resulted in the writing of almost two thousand theoretical treatises in Arabic, Persian, and Turkish. Classical music, because of its intellectual components, is more acceptable. To traditionalists, the most "undesirable" music would be popular styles. [For more information on Middle Eastern attitudes on music, see chapter 3 of *Excursions in World Music* by Nettl et al. (Prentice-Hall, 1992).]

Is there a children's musical culture in Iran?

My impression is that in traditional Iran, children listen to and participate in adult music right from the beginning. In the U.S., there is the notion of children spending more time with other children and less time with adults. In traditional Iran, children associate constantly with parents, grandparents, aunts, uncles, and others within their extended families. Children are often brought along to social events with their parents. Consequently, there is not as much of a need or natural development of a separate children's culture or musical culture in Iran as there is here.

What music do young Iranians learn in school?

There is very little music instruction within the schools in Iran. There were attempts to establish a kind of Western musical style, perhaps largely German-influenced music. Recordings were available for instruction in music appreciation in some schools. But mostly, music does not play very much of a role in the educational system of Iran.

Can you describe something of the traditional approach toward teaching and learning classical Persian music?

In classical Persian music, there is the radif, some three hundred pieces of music, most of them quite short (thirty seconds to four minutes), and they are organized in the twelve modes or dastgāhs. The radif is learned by memorizing it. It takes four years to learn, and some eight to ten hours to play all the way through. At each lesson, the teacher employs oral transmission, singing or playing the material to the student, who sings and plays it back to the teacher. There are many thematic characteristics of each of the twelve dastgāhs and gushehs [phrases of a particular dastgāh, learned by a musician as micromelodies on which improvisation is based] to learn by listening and through much practice. Once the radif is learned, it is *not* performed, but becomes a model, a point of departure, for the musician's improvisation.

What sources can you recommend for teaching classical Persian music—its instruments, cultural functions, and values?

There's so little available. The kind of thing that older students might find useful is the chapter on the Middle East [chapter 3] in *Excursions in World Music* and the tapes that accompany it. The chapter's focus is Iran, improvisation, and the cultural context of music in Iran. It may be useful to teach certain important musical and cultural concepts to students and to provide some guided listening experiences. Understanding Iranian attitudes toward music may be as important as (and more approachable than) attempting to perform it.

What single musical experience in

Lesson Plan for Chanting and Drawing
by Patricia Shehan Campbell

Objectives

Students will:

■ rhythmically chant an Iranian children's rhyme

■ draw while chanting an Iranian children's rhyme

Materials

■ the notated chant (for teacher's use only)

■ chalkboard or large drawing board

■ paper and markers

Procedures

1. Introduce the chant as a popular one learned by young children in Iran. The language is Persian, and the words describe various parts of the body: "chesm" (eyes),

"dahmógho" (nose), "dahan" (mouth), "shecambé" (tummy).

2. Ask the students to keep a steady pulse while you chant the words. Ask students to listen for the descriptive words for the various body parts.

3. Chant again, this time drawing the corresponding body parts on the chalkboard or large drawing board. On the completion of each rhythmic phrase, a bit more of the figure becomes recognizable, until the picture of the little boy (or girl) is revealed at the end of the chant. Repeat the chant, pointing to the body parts that you have drawn.

4. Invite children to join in the chant. Break down the phrases when necessary, although children may learn it best by listening repeatedly to you speaking the chant in its entirety.

5. When children have learned the rhythmic chant, invite them to draw with markers on their papers.

"Chesm, Chesm"

Rhythm:
Pronunciation: Ches-m, ches-m, doh ah-broo,
Text: **Chesm, chesm, doe abru,**
Translation: Eyes, eyes, two eyebrows,

Rhythm:
Pronunciation: Dah-moh-goh, dah-hahn,   yay gehr-doo,
Text: **Dahmógho, dahan, yay gerdoo,**
Translation: One nose, one mouth, one face,

Rhythm:
Pronunciation: Choob, choob, she-cam-bay,
Text: **Chub, chub, shecambé,**
Translation: Side, side, one tummy,

Rhythm:
Pronunciation: In ah-oo-gah chay   gad-dehr gay-shayn - gay
Text: **Ein augha che gadre gashange!**
Translation: What a person—so beautiful!

Source: *Roots and Branches: A Legacy of Multicultural Music for Children,* ©1994 by World Music Press. Used by permission.

Lesson Plan for Listening to the Dastgāh

Objectives

Students will:

- play or sing an approximate rendering of two classical Persian modes, or dastgāhs

- be able to identify several classical Persian instruments (several of which are also found throughout the Middle East)

- identify musical components in two selections of classical Persian music

- imitate and then improvise short phrases based upon the two dastgāhs

Materials

- "Dastgāh Shūr" and "Dastgāh Segāh" from *A Persian Heritage: Classical Music of Iran.* Nonesuch H-72060

- *Musical Instruments of the World,* by the Diagram Group (New York: Facts on File, Inc., 1976)

- listening guide (copies or transparency)

Dastgāh Shūr

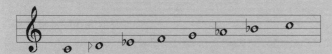

⊅ = 1/4 tone flat

♭ = 1/2 tone flat

Dastgāh Segāh

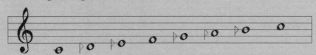

Opening Figure: Dastgāh Segāh

Listening Guides

For "Dastgāh Shūr" (circle one item per line):

Zither (dulcimer)	Bowed lute (fiddle)
Metric: 3/4 meter	Unmetered: free rhythm
Narrow melodic range	Wide melodic range
ABA form	Through-composed form

For "Dastgāh Segāh" (circle one item per line):

Wind instruments/drum/voice	Stringed instruments/drum/voice
Metric: 3/4 meter	Unmetered: free rhythm
Homophonic texture (chordal)	Heterophonic texture (simultaneous melodic variations)
Vocal quality: yodeling	Vocal quality: muted and subdued

by Patricia Shehan Campbell

Procedures

1. Play an approximation of the two modes, the dastgāh shūr and the dastgāh segāh (see music). A violin or cello would best demonstrate the quarter-tone flat (or koron) found in each of the two dastgāhs. Note that dastgāh shūr is close to the Greek Phrygian mode, or the e-e' white-key scale, and note that dastgāh segāh is akin to the major scale, but with quarter-tone flats on the second, third, fifth, sixth, and seventh degrees. Encourage students to attempt to sing the dastgāh.

2. Describe some of the instruments of classical Persian music: the santur (a hammered dulcimer with 72 strings), the tār (a six-stringed lute with a long neck and a skin body that is played with a small plectrum), the kamancha (a four-stringed fiddle with a small skin-covered body that is played vertically with a bow), and the zarb (a wooden, goblet-shaped drum). Refer to the *Musical Instruments of the World* for illustrations. Note that variants of these instruments (especially the zarb) are found throughout the Middle East, from Morocco through Egypt to Turkey.

3. Lead students in playing or singing dastgāh shūr again, and then play about a minute and a half of "Dastgāh Shūr" from the recording. In this initial listening, ask students to direct their attention to the fact that the piece is an improvisation based mostly on the lower four notes (tetrachord) of the dastgāh.

4. Play again the same opening segment of "Dastgāh Shūr." Ask students to use the listening guide (see opposite page) to identify several of the musical components of the excerpt.

5. Lead students in playing or singing dastgāh segāh again, and play the opening instrumental figure. Then play the first minute of "Dastgāh Segāh," a reng or dance-like piece in triple meter, from the recording. Give the translation of the first song: "If you don't comb your hair, your friends will be like your hair—all over the place."

6. Ask students to listen more explicitly to the musical details by using the listening guides. The answers for the "Dastgāh Shūr" are zither, unmetered, wide melodic range, and through-composed form. The answers for the "Dastgāh Segāh" are stringed instruments/drum/voice, metric, heterophonic texture, and vocal quality: yodeling.

7. Compare the students' responses on the listening guides for the two pieces.

8. Following additional listening opportunities, challenge students to improvise upon their choice of dastgāh. Initially, the teacher may present short scale-like phrases and then various rhythmic treatments of three or four pitches of the scale, to be imitated vocally or on instruments. This may be followed by "trading fours," providing opportunities for each student to improvise four-beat micromelodies. Stringed instruments, or even the recorder, would render a slightly more authentic quality than, for example, keyboards or xylophones.

Iranian music should young people have?

An experience with the classical music of Iran may be largely a listening one. Through listening, students can come to terms with a sense of rhythm that is not metric, does not have a steady beat, but does have rhythmic structure. They may also hear pitches that may not appear to sound "in tune" in the Western sense of tuning—pitches that are actually a quarter tone or three-quarter tone flat. As they listen, they may also be led to recognize the cornerstone importance of improvisation within Iranian and nearly all Middle Eastern music. Listening is a sometimes neglected aspect of musical education, but may be especially important in approaching music of the world's cultures.

What should teachers know about teaching Iranian students whom they may have in their classrooms?

Young Iranian people in the U.S. are already tuned in to the notion of studying Western music and culture. We may want to make clear to them that we are interested in their traditional musics and want to learn from them. It would be helpful for all students to have a bit of an acquaintance with the musical heritages of their classmates in order to understand the existence of many complex musical systems.

Do you have any closing remarks regarding the infusion of world music within school music programs?

My general impression is that, rather than teaching musical pieces and styles as individual things to be learned, it would be helpful to integrate these into a larger context of teaching about music of the world. For example, students can know something more about improvisation when they are led to compare the process as undertaken by classical Persian and American jazz musicians. Knowing something about the variety of attitudes and values toward music that are held by people across the world is an important goal, and one that can be integrated into the curriculum at large. ∎

MUSIC IN CULTURAL CONTEXT

ANTHONY SEEGER ON MUSIC OF AMAZONIAN INDIANS

As part of the "Music in Cultural Context" series, this interview with Anthony Seeger focuses on music of communities living in the Amazon river region in Brazil.

BY PATRICIA SHEHAN CAMPBELL

Seeger is an important name in American music. Included among the members of this musical clan are Charles, the distinguished musicologist, Ruth Crawford, the composer and collector of American children's songs, and folk musicians Pete, Mike, and Peggy. Anthony Seeger, grandson of Charles and nephew of Pete, decided early on that, since there were so many members of his family in the music business, he would do something different: become an anthropologist. He is known today as a prominent anthropologist, ethnomusicologist, and archivist, and he maintains the strong connection to music that his family has had for several generations.

Anthony Seeger heard his first non-Western music "in the womb" and discovered the music of India while he was learning about Indian history in the sixth grade. He wrote a paper on African music in the eighth grade and a paper on Japanese music in the ninth grade, using as sources the Folkways records he had searched out in stores in Manhattan, where he grew

Anthony Seeger

Photo by Rick Vargas

up. A banjo player since he was ten, Seeger still plays today—in his Washington, D.C., home or in a Brazilian Suyá village.

Seeger received his bachelor's degree from Harvard University and his master's and doctoral degrees in anthropology from the University of

Chicago. His research has concentrated on the cosmology, social organization, and music of the Amazonian Indians. His books include *Nature and Society in Central Brazil: The Suyá Indians of Mato Grosso* (Cambridge: Harvard University Press, 1981) and *Why Suyá Sing: A Musical Anthropology of an Amazonian People* (Cambridge: Cambridge University Press, 1987). He lived in Brazil for nearly ten years, for much of that time as a member of the graduate faculty of the Department of Anthropology at the National Museum in Rio de Janeiro.

In 1982, Seeger returned to the U.S. as associate professor of anthropology and director of the Indiana University Archives of Traditional Music. In 1988, he moved to the Smithsonian Institution to assume the direction of Folkways Records and to become the curator of the archival collection of the Center for Folklife Programs and Cultural Studies. In the last seven years, he has produced more than one hundred recordings. He is a fellow of the American Academy of Arts and Sciences and was president of the Society for Ethnomusicology from 1992 to 1994.

Here are Seeger's responses to questions about music of the Amazon river region and the world at large.

Patricia Shehan Campbell is professor in the School of Music at the University of Washington in Seattle and chair of the Society for Ethnomusicology's Education Committee.

MUSIC IN CULTURAL CONTEXT

When, where, and how should world musics be taught?

Music from different parts of the world should be introduced into the curriculum at the earliest possible moment. It can be used as part of musical activities or as part of world studies and history. I do not think it should be kept isolated in the music curriculum. It is partly a question of ear training and partly a question of approach.

If children know that there are a lot of different types of music out there in the world, their early exposure will at least get them started listening for the different types. We should give up some of the space and time currently given for Western art music in order to teach other musics. We no longer only teach U.S. and state history; we also include new physics and new biology in our science courses. By including more of the world's musics in our music curriculum, we do not abandon the Western musics but rather place them in perspective.

What recommendations do you have for teachers who wish further knowledge of musics other than that of their own earlier training?

There are an increasing number of avenues through which to get access to information about world music for teachers. There are college textbooks with recordings and special teachers' packages put together by MENC and National Public Radio. [The packages are collectively called *Sounds of the World* and include individual cassettes and teachers' guides for music of Eastern Europe, Latin America, East Asia, the Middle East, and Southeast Asia.]

There are an increasing number of on-line bulletin boards that put teachers in touch with each other and let them share information about their programs and ask for and give help. Video materials are appearing, and more audio recordings than ever are becoming available. Local colleges sometimes give courses. The journal *Ethnomusicology* provides reviews of books, recordings, and videotapes.

And there are often concerts or presentations by non-Western musicians or local immigrants at local folk festivals. I recommend going out to meet people and, if they live locally, asking

■ ■ ■ ■ ■ ■

Music and dance are identified by the same word — "ngere"—and song and movement are almost always connected in some significant way.

■ ■ ■ ■ ■ ■

them to participate in the classroom experience. Try finding musicians among school parents, too.

Do you differentiate between the terms "traditional" and "authentic"?

There is a difference, but its importance depends on our approach to the music. What are we using the music to teach? If we are using the music to teach about vocal quality in different cultures, then it is important to distinguish music that was historically identified with a community (traditional) from music that has been introduced (nontraditional, yet authentic), possibly through missionization or military enforcement. However, if we are teaching for understanding of a musical element like cross-rhythms, it doesn't

Figure 1. Xingu region (boxed area) of Brazil

matter how authentic a certain piece of Afro-pop may be if that particular piece has no cross-rhythms in it.

Are children and youth becoming exposed to the world's musics through the media's transmission of "world pop"?

There is a difference between "world pop" and the full spectrum of the music of different countries. Most of the world's popular music has a steady drum beat and electric instrumentation. The fact that children may be listening to "world pop" is a positive thing, but there are other musical styles to learn, too. Even if children listen to the Boston Pops at home, they are exposed to just one dimension of Western art music. School music programs can offer children musical experiences that extend what they know from the home and from the media.

What is the musical culture of your own expertise?

I am a specialist in the musical performances of the Brazilian Indian communities in the Amazon River region. There are virtually no practitioners of this culture in the U.S. because the Indians rarely leave the area. The group with which I have worked most intensively is the Suyá Indians.

Where do the Suyá live?

In 1972 when my fieldwork began, the Suyá Indians lived in a single circular village with seven houses and a population of about one hundred and twenty in the Parque Indigena do Xingu in Mato Grosso, Brazil (see figure 1). Today they live in a much larger village, which is a day's paddle upstream from their old site. The village has fifteen houses, a population of about one hundred and eighty, and ambitious plans for the future. It is located on a large bend in the Suiá-missu River, in the midst of subsistence resources.

There are rivers and lakes rich with fish (though the Suyá are concerned about how muddy the water has become with settlers living upstream) and ample forests for hunting jaguars, tapirs, wild pigs, forest deer, and other

■ ■ ■ ■ ■ ■

Among the Suyá and other lowland peoples of South America, it appears that whenever music is heard, something important is happening.

■ ■ ■ ■ ■ ■

game animals as well as for making gardens. The staple crop, manioc, grows well in the rich earth near the Suyá's current village, as do bananas, corn, and sweet potatoes. [Manioc is a tuber that grows in all kinds of soils, and preparing it is quite time-consuming. Because of its poisonous acid, it has to be grated, washed, dried, and then cooked before it can be eaten.]

The village has a large, hard-packed central plaza, a ring of residential houses, and gardens on three sides with the river on the fourth. The village has a center and a periphery; it is a social system unto itself. Today, of course, the Suyá are hooked into the rest of the country—a solar panel powers a two-way radio that they use to speak with other Indians, to send messages to the Indian bureau, and to

■■■■ *North American Songs for* ■■■■
South American Suyá

"Let's sing," a man says when I reach the group of men, carrying my stool. "All right, let's sing," I reply. "No, let's sing YOUR songs," corrects another. "All right." Even though we are feeling heavy from eating a lot of starch, I return to the house and tell Judy the men want us to sing. When we take our banjo and guitar into the center of the plaza, the women follow us and form a ring of women and children around the men at the center.

Judy and I have played and sung folk music for many years, but the experience of playing for the Suyá is different from any other. We begin with a Bluegrass style banjo song, "John Hardy," and follow it with another in close parallel harmony and a modal tuning, "Pretty Polly." The women have been asking Judy to teach them some songs privately. They know the first verse of "Pretty Polly" in English, and join in. Then we sing two audience participation songs from Africa, "Tina Singu Lelo Votaeo" and "Bayeza." After all of the months we have been living with them, the Suyá sing these enthusiastically....They like "Michael Row the Boat Ashore" because it sounds like "Wai kum kraw," or "Look out, something is rotten smelling." They are generally uninterested in translations. They sing songs in a number of different Indian languages which they do not understand. Ours is just another set of different sounds and a different vocal style.

Source: Anthony Seeger, *Why Suyá Sing: A Musical Anthropology of an Amazonian People* (Cambridge: Cambridge University Press, 1987), pp. 19-20. Reprinted by permission. ©1987 by Cambridge University Press.

Suyá Indians perform a ritual dance with song.

Veil," and "Bayeza." We had such a good time that we all want to go back next year for another visit—but first we have to learn some new songs.

Among the Suyá, what is the meaning and function of music and dance?

Music and dance are identified by the same word—"ngere"—and song and movement are almost always connected in some significant way. Among the Suyá and other lowland peoples of South America, it appears that whenever music is heard, something important is happening. Usually some connection is being created or re-created between different domains of life, the universe, or the human body and its spirits.

All Suyá music is vocal, although neighboring Amazonian Indian communities perform on a large number of wind instruments. Music is also related to myths and to Suyá ideas of history. The village is a kind of concert hall, the year is a kind of concert, with spaced performances that are related to each other, and the society is a kind of orchestra—songs and vocal styles are determined by age and gender, not biology.

consult with medical doctors in Sao Paulo as needed.

Who are the Suyá?

They are a lowland South American tribal people who live by hunting, fishing, and planting and sowing the fruits of their gardens. They vary in appearance. There are older men with long hair, large wooden lip disks in their lower lips, and empty loops of earlobe hanging and flapping. There are young men with Upper Xingu Indian bowl-style haircuts and no lip ornaments. They wear an assortment of tattered shorts and shirts, except when they sing; then they take off their clothes, paint their bodies, and dance and sing without clothes. There are women in faded knee-length dresses who work at processing manioc tubers, tend their children, and talk unceasingly among themselves. [A history of the Suyá and other Ge-speaking people of the Mato Grosso can be found in Seeger's *Nature and Society in Central Brazil.*]

Have you visited the Suyá recently?

Last summer, my wife, two daughters (ages fifteen and seventeen), and I returned to the Suyá for the first time since 1982. We went back to see how they were, to videotape dance movements (a task that was impossible before solar-powered battery chargers), and to give them video equipment, with solar panels and rechargeable batteries, to enable them to document their own culture as well as invasions of their land and rivers.

They received us enthusiastically, proudly showed us their new village and its surroundings, as well as their songs and dances, and asked for our assistance in a number of long-range projects. We sang for each other repeatedly. My wife and I joined in some Suyá songs and movements with the adults. The Suyá youth enthusiastically learned cheers and the electric slide from our younger daughter, while the older people joined in on some of our old stand-bys for the first time in over a decade: "Pretty Polly," "Long Black

What is the single "most representative music" among the Suyá?

There are two principal genres of music: a low unison song sung by adult men and individual shout-songs sung by men and boys. In the latter, all of the adult men and children sing different melodies, but dance to a single rhythm. Women accompany men in ceremonial dancing but do not sing (they only dance); they are important as an audience for men's singing. The women perform Suyá women's songs when working together. They have their own ceremonies that feature songs and dances, many of which were videotaped by my wife and daughters this past summer.

How has the music of the Suyá changed from what it once was?

No one (from the outside) heard Suyá music before 1959 or so, so no one can tell how it has changed. The Suyá like to learn music from other societies, and they have been adding new traditions to their repertory for

Lesson Plan for Songs for Seasons and Ceremonies

by Patricia Shehan Campbell

Objectives

Students will:

- explain the importance of singing in Amazonian Indian cultures
- keep the pulse while listening to Amazonian Indian songs
- describe the vocal timbre and identify the pitch components of Amazonian Indian song
- portray through paints, markers, or crayons characters and scenarios of an Amazonian Indian song

Materials

- "Rainy Season" unison song from cassette tape that accompanies Anthony Seeger's *Why Suyá Sing* (Cambridge: Cambridge University Press, 1987). Cassette available through Center for Folklife Programs, Smithsonian Institution, Washington, D.C.*
- "No'ōk-āmōr" from *Voices of Forgotten Worlds* (Roslyn, NY: Ellipsis Arts, 1993), a book with two CDs*
- rattle
- notated music (see below)
- paper (canvas), paints, markers, crayons

*This selection may be featured alone in a lesson or in conjunction with the other recording.

Procedures

1. Set the scene for the Suyá "Rainy Season" unison song. Explain how, based on Seeger's description, the men sit together in the men's house and, as they sing, hit their right fists on their thighs. The song is a fish song, and its translation is "The trairao fish sings with its face painted for log racing. Huu, with its face painted sings, huu, huu. The big-mouth bass sings with body painted for log-racing." There are "song words" (jo-jo-ha-i) interspersed that are not directly translatable.

Body painting and face painting are important in preparation for ceremonies, including the combination of ceremony and sport when men run relay races carrying heavy logs into the village. In this song, the "fish" take on human characteristics by having painted faces and running in log races.

2. Set the scene for the Kayapo "No'ōk-āmōr." Explain how the Kayapo live in villages scattered along the Xingu River, not far from the Suyá. Despite their contacts with gold miners, rubber workers, Brazil-nut gatherers, hunters, and land speculators, the Kayapo maintain much of their ceremonial life. As corn is the staple food of the rainy season, many important rituals surround it. Bayjangri, the corn festival, is celebrated each year for a period of three months, from the first appearance of the seedlings to the harvest of the corn.

The corn festival song featured on the CD is taken from a rehearsal for the ceremony, conducted by the Kayapo elders, who arrange the verses and the movement. The stops and starts are heard, with breaks in between the verses. Some of the younger Kayapo men record the rehearsals on tape, in order to listen to and practice the songs at home.

3. Play the opening segments of the recordings—if you cannot obtain both recordings, one will do. Keep the pulse by tapping the fist on the thigh. Then, ask students to use the rattle to keep the beat.

4. Play the opening segments of the recordings again. Ask students to listen for the quality of the voices (male voices in their lowest registers).

5. Follow the notation of the opening phrases (song words) of the Suyá "Rainy Season" unison song (see below) while listening, noting the frequent recurrence of the three pitches.

6. Listen to the Kayapo "No'ōk-āmōr" for the use of just three pitches: *do, fa, sol.* Listen for the sometimes quick and sometimes sustained rhythms of these pitches.

7. Depict the log-rolling contest, the painted face and body of the fish (Suyá), and the corn ceremony (Kayapo), using paints, markers, and crayons.

Source: "Rainy Season" unison song, transcribed by Marina Roseman in Anthony Seeger, *Why Suyá Sing: A Musical Anthropology of an Amazonian People* (Cambridge: Cambridge University Press, 1987). Used by permission.©1987 by Cambridge University Press.

Lesson Plan for "Why Suyá Sing?"

by Patricia Shehan Campbell

Objectives

Students will:

- ask questions of themselves and others pertinent to music making as a fundamental human endeavor, a universal need that extends across all cultures
- describe the importance of song in the lives of the Suyá people
- compare the role and function of music among the Suyá with their own musical needs and interests

Materials

- blackboard/drawing easel
- paper and pen/pencil

Procedures

1. Ask students, "Is music important to you? Why? How?"

2. Show photographs of Amazonian peoples. Black and white photographs are found in Seeger's *Nature and Society in Central Brazil* and *Why Suyá Sing*. Color photographs of the Kayapo can be found in *Voices of Forgotten Worlds* from Ellipsis Arts. The photos accompanying this article can also be used.

3. As a class, list and discuss the functions and precepts of music among the Suyá people. (Refer to Seeger's *Why Suyá Sing* for further information.) The functions and precepts include the following:

- The body is used as an instrument in Suyá singing ceremonies and celebrations. Suyá song is a physical as well as a social experience, and singing is thus intimately connected to rigorous movement and dance.
- Song types and singing (or the absence of singing) are associated with particular moods and sentiments of the Suyá. Ceremonies and seasons bring about song. But an angry person, or a sad person in mourning, does not sing. A person in the middle of a political dispute might sing for a short time, and then return to his house, revealing his discontent and lack of euphoria.
- Among the Suyá, singing is part of social reproduction, an integral part of the rites of passage that order a person's life.
- Suyá songs attest to the continued interaction of humans and animals. Specialists among the Suyá hear natural species sing, and teach their songs to the people.
- In Suyá society, music—singing and dancing—is not an option but an obligation. Even though only a few people are designated to speak openly in public oratory, everyone participates in the music making.

4. In small groups, students can discuss how the Suyá precepts hold meaning for them. A recorder can be designated to take notes. The following questions may help to guide the discussion:

- How is singing a physical experience for you? Do you sing while you dance?
- Depending upon your mood, do you sing or play or listen to some music more than others? Do you choose music to reflect how you are feeling?
- Did you sing some songs when you were preschool age or in elementary school that you do not sing now?
- How are the bird calls and cries very much like songs? Do you know any bird calls, cries, or songs?
- Is music making important to you? To people, generally?

5. Share the small-group reflections with the class at large. Take notes for later discussion.

A Suyá woman anoints a package of fish that will be carried back to the village in a ritual relay race.

Photo by Anthony Seeger

hundreds of years. Since 1959, they have learned a few songs in Portuguese, a few from my wife and me in English and some African languages, a few from our daughters, and others from Indians they had never met before. What has affected their singing more recently is the death of a large proportion of the members of their society during raids and epidemics, which makes them sad and less interested in singing.

What music do Suyá children make?

Children perform adults' music. Either they do so as part of ceremonies, or they have their own ceremonies after the adults are finished, playing down by the river. Most interesting were some ceremonies organized *by* the children *for* the children, such as one where a group of five- to eight-year-old boys went out fishing and brought back a small catch to be shared with some young girls, after which they sang. Suyá children learn music from the adults in the community, their peers, and to some extent from radios and cassette tapes. The radios play Brazilian popular music, and the tapes are often filled with Suyá ceremonies and music of other Brazilian Indian groups.

Can music of the Amazonian Indians be taught in American schools?

This would be very difficult. There is very little information about Amazonian Indian music, and little of what exists is particularly appropriate for children. [The lesson plans accompanying this article were reviewed and endorsed by Seeger as "good ways to work with this music."]

In general, what would you suggest as introductory experiences in the world's musical cultures for children?

Regarding the music curriculum, I would recommend exposing children to a wide (not necessarily multitudinous) variety of approaches to sounds. With four or five different examples, many of the world's musical sounds and concepts can be introduced. Music should also be included within the world studies curriculum. When children are studying India, for example, they might be led to experiences

A Suyá man makes a rattle by stringing fruit pits on a long cord.

with Indian music. The same can be said for musical experiences to accompany their study of Brazil and the Amazonian rain forest. When they study slavery, they might be taught to listen and then to emulate the sounds of field hollers. When they study immigration, they might be directed to an understanding of Cambodian and Vietnamese music—as it sounded in the homeland and as it has changed over time in the U.S.

In performing the musics of the world's cultures, what special sensitivities should teachers and students develop?

Generally, performers should choose nonreligious materials, or at least, verify that performing religious music would not be offensive to the originating communities. Performances of musical arrangements should be acknowledged as such, and arrangers should state that they are approximating but not actually duplicating the performances. Translations of the texts should be provided whenever possible. All performers

should be exposed at some point to the "authentic" performance of the piece or genre. [The music of the first lesson plan is linked to ceremonies laden with spiritual significance, but because it is not primarily "religious" it can be studied and sung outside of its original context.]

What world musics are better off not performed?

Much religious music—of any culture—should probably remain out of the realm of school performances. Also, some concert music where performers are trained in conservatories for many years should be left for only those students who are well versed in those traditions.

What closing words of advice can you offer to musician-educators?

Music should be fun to listen to and to make. We should not be embarrassed about trying to do new things, as long as we remember to pay respect to musical traditions and homage to the great musicians of those traditions. ■

MUSIC IN CULTURAL CONTEXT

BELL YUNG ON MUSIC OF CHINA

As part of the "Music in Cultural Context" series, this interview with Bell Yung focuses on the music of China.

BY PATRICIA SHEHAN CAMPBELL

Bell Yung was born in Shanghai, China, in 1941, at a time of great national change—the period between the demise of the last dynasty and the rise and official establishment of the communist People's Republic of China. China was both traditional and changing then, and his early musical memories reflect the blend of Chinese and Western cultures in China that was so typical of the times: "I loved to sing, and I was not shy. I remember standing on the family's dining-room table, singing Chinese folk songs and songs made popular on Chinese radio and through movies. ... I also remember my aunt playing the piano. I'd listen to her, and then imitate later on what she had played."

When Yung was a young schoolchild, his family moved to Hong Kong. There he began to pursue serious study of the piano, particularly the repertoire and technique of the nineteenth-century European master composers. All around him, however, were

Patricia Shehan Campbell is professor in the School of Music at the University of Washington in Seattle and chair of the Society for Ethnomusicology's Education Committee.

Bell Yung

Photo courtesy of the author

the sounds of Chinese instruments, opera, narrative songs, and music of the street festivals and temples.

In 1960, Yung came to the United States to attend college. He received a bachelor of science degree in engineering physics from the University of California at Berkeley. He then went on to complete a doctorate in physics from the Massachusetts Institute of Technol-

ogy and a doctorate in music from Harvard University. As he explains: "I liked music, but I also did well in science. There is a certain perspective in China, as well as in the U.S., that if a person can 'do' science, he should. I often thought of switching from science to music, but didn't want to waste the fellowships. Finally, when I finished at MIT, I asked myself, 'What do I really want to do?' So, without hesitation, I walked down the road to Harvard. In interesting ways, my physics career has some deeply rooted influence over how I think and how I formulate musical problems."

He is now professor of music at the University of Pittsburgh, where he teaches courses in ethnomusicology and historical musicology. He has also taught at Cornell University, the Chinese University of Hong Kong, and the University of California at Davis.

Known internationally as a leading scholar of Chinese music, Yung is author of *Cantonese Opera: Performance as Creative Process* (Cambridge University Press, 1989) and *Celestial Airs of Antiquity: Music of the Seven-String Zither of China* (AR Editions, 1995). His articles on Cantonese opera, guqin (a seven-string zither; pronounced "goo-CHIN"), and Chinese singers and songs have appeared in publications from Japan, Switzerland, the People's Republic of China, Taiwan, Hong Kong, and in journals such as *Ethnomusicology, JAMS,* and *Chinoperl Papers* in the U.S. He is currently working on a book about blind singers of southern China, coediting (with Evelyn S. Rawski and Rubie S. Watson) a volume of essays titled *Harmony and Counterpoint: Ritual Music in Chinese Context* (Stanford University Press), and coediting (with Yoshihiko Tokumaru and Robert Provine) the East and Inner Asia volume of the *Garland Encyclopedia of World Music.* He is the founder and director of the Association for Chinese Music Research.

A performer as well as a scholar, Yung has given recitals on the Chinese guqin. In recent years, he has returned often to Shanghai and Hong Kong for research on this instrument and on Cantonese opera and narrative songs. He has also conducted fieldwork in Indonesia and has studied and performed on the gamelan. For all of his diverse musical knowledge, he chooses to play Schubert and Brahms on the piano—"for relaxation."

Here are Yung's answers to questions about music of China and the world at large.

When, where, and why should world musics be taught?

World musics (or multicultural music) should be taught as early as possible, in schools as well as at home. The reasons for this are much more significant than many people realize: (a) to increase the students' knowledge of and sensitivity to music, and (b) to acknowledge and honor the multicultural components of the American population and the multicultural nature of the world's people. We must recognize that Western art music is not music with a capital M but merely one kind of music. In American society at large and outside of the classroom, Western art music is quite accessible through concerts, radio and television broadcasts, and commercial cassettes and CDs, and is a close relative (rhythmically, tonally, and harmonically) to the widely available popular music. Comparatively, non-Western music is much less available

and must be given a special "sell" in order to have equal playing time. The place to do this is in the schools.

What rationale relevant to larger societal issues can be offered for teaching the world's musics?

A more fundamental and important reason for teaching the world's musics should also be put forward. With all the conflicts among people in the world today, be it conflicts based upon race, ethnicity, religious beliefs, or nationality, the core of the problem is one of ignorance and alienation and fear of the unknown "other" who is different from us. We fear what we don't know and what we are not familiar with. We dream up all kinds of horrors in association with the "other." But if we can put a face on the "other," such alienation is lessened. One of the most conveniently learned faces of the

"other" is his or her music. Since everyone loves music (one's own), it is easy to accept that other people also love music, even the spooky "other." Knowing the kind of music the "other" loves must undoubtedly make the distance between strangers a little smaller, add a little more familiarity, and make the "other" more human and more like oneself.

The whole concept of racial integration in schools, if I understand it correctly, is based upon this same idea: through familiarity and day-to-day contact, children will get used to each other's presence and will get to know each other's language, behavior, and habits, resulting in decreased suspicion and fear. Of course, racism and bigotry have much more complex roots and reasons, but promoting more direct contacts cannot but help to move us in the right direction. The next best thing to direct physical contact is exposure to

Figure 1. China and surrounding area

various cultural expressions of the people. Music is a very convenient way of achieving that end.

How can musics of the world's cultures be offered to children, especially when teachers have limited time?

I strongly believe that exposing children to the sound of music at an early age is important—to get them used to the sound so that it is no longer unusual and "weird." Therefore, selections of world musics can be offered as background in many settings. Familiarity with the world's musical traditions, even without any understanding, is better than total alienation. Children may not need to be exposed to a great variety of foreign music. Even one musical style from one other culture will be enough to give them a new perspective, a world view. It will open up their ears and make them aurally less provincial.

Can children's exposure to "world pop" on radio, television, and videotapes be interpreted to show there is a lesser need for instruction in world music?

Not really. "World pop" has essentially one single, homogenized sound, while traditional and art music of the world's peoples more genuinely reflect the rich variety of musics around the world. "World pop" is relatively easily available on radio, television, and videotape, while traditional musics are not.

Given classroom time constraints, how can teachers and their students be trained in musical styles that are different from those of their earlier experience?

The University of Pittsburgh addresses this issue through its development of an outreach program to local high schools and elementary schools. Two approaches are taken: (a) traditional musicians travel to the schools to perform for students, and (b) special workshops on music of particular cultures are arranged for teachers, with materials disseminated to them for classroom use.

What is your view of the use and meaning of "authentic" and "traditional" in reference to musics of world cultures?

I almost never use "authentic" to discuss the music of China because it implies absolute values that, in most cases, do not exist. To me, authenticity is little more than an arbitrary construct to serve political purposes. Let me explain what I mean. First, it is very difficult to objectively prove authenticity. In most cases of Chinese music, if one traces the history of a musical genre or a musical instrument far enough back in time, one inevitably encounters different influences upon its development, some of which were "foreign." Some of the most well-known Chinese musical instruments such as the pipa and erh-hu have well-known foreign origins. Are these instruments still authentic or less authentic? Where is one to draw the cut-off line in time so that one can disregard foreign influence?

■ ■ ■ ■ ■ ■

Children may not need to be exposed to a great variety of foreign music. Even one musical style … will be enough to give them a new perspective.

■ ■ ■ ■ ■ ■

Secondly, if one were to use the "native's" judgment as a gauge for authenticity, one also encounters problems. There are so many kinds of Chinese music, catering to so many kinds of Chinese people. What is considered to be authentic by some Chinese may not be so to others. Who is to judge? Furthermore, one would also

encounter the problem of deciding who is or is not an authentic Chinese. China is made up of a heterogeneous people with differences among some groups as great as those between any two groups of people in the world. Furthermore, as we well know, many Chinese, through the centuries, have immigrated to all parts of the world, to Southeast Asia in particular but also to North America in large numbers in recent decades. Many of them still identify with China, yet their understanding of China is quite different from the reality of China today. Who is the authentic Chinese?

What is the musical culture of your expertise?

There are three facets to my research of Chinese music. The first is Chinese opera, specifically Cantonese opera of southern China (one of about 350 different kinds of regional theaters). Cantonese opera has been performed in the U.S. since the mid-nineteenth century, following the arrival of Chinese immigrants. Today, there are Cantonese opera clubs in major cities such as San Francisco and New York. Visiting troupes from Hong Kong also regularly perform in major U.S. cities having large numbers of Cantonese immigrants—people originally from the southern province of Guangdong. Peking opera activities are also found, with performance and training possibilities, in several U.S. cities. Since the 1980s, a significant number of professional opera performers have immigrated to the U.S., offering high-caliber performances. This is a great resource.

My second research interest is Chinese narrative songs, specifically those of southern China that are sung in Cantonese. These include refined poetry as well as popular, even vulgar, songs performed in teahouses or brothels. This kind of singing is dying out rapidly in China. A small number of singers now live in the U.S. See the videotape *Singing to Remember* (Asian American Arts Center, New York, 1992) about an eighty-year-old, narrative-song singer now living in New York.

The third facet of my research is instrumental music, particularly that of the seven-string zither called guqin. This instrument is one of the oldest musical instruments in China and is a very refined instrument associated with the literati class. A small number of guqin players live in the U.S. Other Chinese instrumentalists [among them, players of a plucked lute called pipa (pronounced "PEE-pah"), a transverse flute called dixi (pronounced "DEE-tsuh"), a two-string fiddle called erh-hu (pronounced "EHR-hoo"), and a hammered dulcimer called yang qin (pronounced "yahng-CHIN")] have also recently immigrated from China, providing another great resource.

Within Chinese culture, what is the function of the musical genres you have mentioned?

Chinese opera has two major social functions: entertainment and ritual. In recent years, the entertainment value is more prominent. Narrative songs and instrumental music serve mainly as entertainment. Chinese opera is, of course, related to theater. It is a source of great inspiration for dance and visual arts (costumes and face painting), just as it has also been inspired by the arts, ancient legends, and classic literature. Both opera and narrative songs are an important source for Chinese folk literature.

Within this musical culture, what music is the single "most representative music"?

This is a very difficult question. The three kinds of music I've just mentioned are representative of China. Among them, the operas (and, to a lesser extent, narrative songs) are probably the most important because the different kinds cater to people of all classes and ages, in almost all parts of China. And operas are tied closely to the history and folklore of China. However, since vocal music is always more difficult for the noninitiated to appreciate, I would suggest focusing on instrumental music, particularly those types that are more easily palatable to Americans. If I were to choose one kind of Chinese music for children, I would choose instrumental music even though it is not necessarily more representative. Among the types of instrumental music, I would say

solo music of the erh-hu, guzheng (plucked, bridged zither; pronounced "goo-JUNG"), xiao (vertical flute; pronounced "SHAHW"), and Jiangnan Sizhu (a silk and bamboo instrumental ensemble; pronounced "jee-AHNG-nahn SEE-joo"). [Note: There is also the accessible music of the drum and gong ensembles, generically referred to as luogu (pronounced "lu-OH-goo")].

How is Chinese music today different from what it was at an earlier time?

Chinese music today retains some traditional elements of its long past, but it has undergone a great deal of change in the last century, mainly because Chinese society has changed

so greatly. Take instrumental music as an example. Changes include the construction of musical instruments (silk strings are mostly replaced by metal and nylon strings), the performance style (being more uniform throughout the country rather than having many distinctive styles from one region to another), compositional techniques (consciously composed music rather than tunes handed down for generations), the use of notation rather than oral transmission, and concert performance for large groups rather than small audiences. Yet, much of the repertory is still traditional because of deeper forms of the compositions and performance techniques—historically

---

▬ *Selected Recordings of Chinese Music* ▬

Folk Songs

Vocal Music of Contemporary China. Volume 1: The Han People. Ethnic Folkways FE4091.

Opera

The Chinese Opera. Lyrichord LLST7212 (Peking opera).

Chinese Opera: Songs and Music. Folkways 8880 (Cantonese opera).

Instrumental Music

A Musical Anthology of the Orient: China. UNESCO Collection: Muscaphon BM30 SL2032 (qin, zheng, pipa).

Chinese Masterpieces for the Erh-hu. Lyrichord LLST7132.

Music of the Chinese Pipa. Nonesuch H72085.

Chinese Instruments: An Anthology of the World's Music. Anthology Records AST-4000 (pipa, qin, sanxian, yangqin, zheng).

Spring Night on a Moonlit River. Nonesuch 72089 (zheng).

Lesson Plan for Chinese Festival Music

by Patricia Shehan Campbell

Objectives

Students will:

- become acquainted with Chinese festivals and the music associated with them
- play a brief festival piece on gongs and drums

Materials

- hand cymbals (any size)
- drums (timpani, conga, played with mallets)
- gongs, bells, woodblocks
- *The Lion's Roar: Chinese Luogu Percussion Ensembles* by Han Kuo-Huang and Patricia Shehan Campbell (Danbury, CT: World Music Press, 1992), including book, tape, slides
- *The Chinese New Year* by Cheng Hou-tien (New York: Holt, Rinehart, and Winston, 1976)

Procedures

1. Recall with students the part that music plays in American holiday celebrations, particularly in parades on Memorial Day, the Fourth of July, and Thanksgiving. Explain that traditional Chinese festivals at New Year's Day (Guo Nian) and throughout the year (the Lantern Festival, the Clear and Bright Festival, the Dragon Boat Festival, and the Double Seventh Festi-

val, for example) also feature music. Note that the rousing music of such festivals is invariably loud and rhythmic and features instruments—drums, gongs, cymbals—that may seldom be played indoors.

2. Introduce "Shehuo Gudien" (pronounced "SHUH-hoo-oh GOO-dee-ehn"), or "Festival Rhythm," a piece originating in northwestern China. The music is associated with the agricultural cycle of transplanting and is performed at the season of New Year, between late January and mid-February, and during harvest time. Players of drums and gongs in the luogu ensemble dress in elaborate costumes and march through the streets, alongside bright red lanterns decorated with fringe. They make their way to a central park or plaza, where the music and dancing continues.

3. Chant the mnemonic syllables in rhythm (shown below).

4. Slowly increase the chant speed. Students may also pat on "chay," clap on "chahng," and wave their hands outward (to indicate silence, or rest) on "ee."

5. Add instruments. Only hand cymbals play on the "chay," but all instruments (cymbals, drums, gongs, bells, woodblock) play on "chahng." As students grasp the rhythm and percussive techniques, the spoken chant can be gradually faded away.

6. While the piece can be played continually in a parade, it can be ended through a rhythmic signal played by the drum in the last measure. See below.

"Festival Rhythm"

chay chay   chay chay   chahng   ee   chay chay   chay chay   chahng   ee

chay chay   chay chay   chahng   chahng

chay chahng   chay chahng   chay chay

chahng   chay   chahng   ee

Rhythmic signal to end "Festival Rhythm"

dong dong dong dong   dong dong dong   ee

Lesson Plan for Chinese Instrumental Music

Objectives

Students will:

- listen to short recorded examples of traditional Chinese instrumental music

- identify and describe instruments and musical components in the examples

- compose a piece in the style of Chinese traditional music for recorder (or flute) and woodblock

Materials

- recording of *China: Shantung Folk Music and Traditional Instrumental Pieces* (Nonesuch H-72051)

- *Musical Instruments of the World* by the Diagram Group (New York: Facts on File, Inc., 1976)

- listening guide (copies or transparency), shown below

- recorder, woodblock

Procedures

1. Explain that, due to China's great geographic expanse, long history, and cultural diversity, there is no single style that represents Chinese music. Instead, there are many genres of folk music, court music, ancient ritual music, opera, entertainment music, and solo and ensemble music. Each region has its preferred musical instruments, ensembles, melodies, characteristic rhythms, and performance techniques—and sometimes these will vary from one city or town to the next. The music of this lesson comes from Shantung, a province of northeast China, and includes both classical and folk examples of program music (expressive of a particular theme or image) and "pure" music.

2. Refer to *Musical Instruments of the World* for illustrations of some of the best known instruments from throughout China: the erh-hu (two-string fiddle), sometimes called nanhu (pronounced "NAN-hoo"); zheng (sixteen-string plucked zither; pronounced "JUHNG"), sometimes called guzheng; dixi (transverse flute); sheng (seventeen-tube bamboo mouth organ; pronounced "SHUHNG"); and pipa

(plucked lute). Note that these instruments are played either solo or in combination in small ensembles or large orchestras. They can be played in concert or to accompany opera or dance.

3. Provide students with brief (1–2 minute) listening examples in order that they may become acquainted with well-known musical instruments and style characteristics. Guide them in attentive listening. In "Beautiful Spring," have them listen for these features:

- zheng solo

- ascending and descending glissandi

- bending and sliding of pitches

- free rhythm, eventually becoming metered

- treble and bass strings, often playing the melody in octaves

- syncopated melody (including the pattern of dotted quarter note, eighth note, quarter note, quarter note).

In "Chirping of a Hundred Birds," have them listen for these features:

- dixi, with nanhu, sheng, and bangzi (woodblock; pronounced "BAHNG-zee")

- dixi trills and flourishes

- dixi in scalar and arpeggiated passages

- free rhythm, eventually becoming metered

- dixi melody leaping from lower to higher octave

- quickening pace, emphasized by double-time bangzi.

4. Ask students to listen to two additional examples, "Moonlit Night" (played on nanhu) and "A Fair Lady and a Cowherd" (played on dixi). Have them select appropriate descriptions of the musical content on the listening guides provided on the next page. (The descriptions that fit "Moonlit Night" are string, monophonic, embellished melody, large pitch range, pentatonic, and duple meter. The descriptions that

fit "A Fair Lady and a Cowherd" are wind, monophonic, embellished melody, large pitch range, pentatonic, and free rhythm that becomes metered.)

5. Repeat listening as necessary so that students may check their responses and come to terms with common musical characteristics. Several common components should emerge: pentatonic melodies (in particular, d-r-m-s-l), duple meter with an introductory free-rhythm section, melodic embellishments such as passing tones (tones or pitches between the principal pitches of a melody) or trills, wide ranges (two octaves or more), and rhythmic syncopation. Call their attention to the programmatic titles of the pieces, and note how musical components express these themes.

6. Divide students into pairs or small groups. Assign them the task of composing a piece in the style of traditional Chinese music. Parameters may include a pentatonic scale in G and rhythms consisting of four quarter notes; two quarter notes and a half note; a dotted quarter note, eighth note, and two quarter notes; and an eighth note, quarter note, eighth note, and quarter note. An ostinato accompaniment can be added on woodblock. Students may wish to give programmatic titles to their pieces and perform them for each other.

Photo courtesy of the author

The preeminent guqin musician, Mrs. Cai Deyun (née Florence Shen) of Hong Kong.

Listening Guides

"Moonlit Night"		"A Fair Lady and a Cowherd"	
wind	string	wind	string
monophonic	chordal	monophonic	chordal
"straight" plain melody	embellished melody	"straight" plain melody	embellished melody
small pitch range	large pitch range	small pitch range	large pitch range
pentatonic	diatonic	pentatonic	diatonic
duple meter	triple meter	free rhythm that becomes metered	metered, changing meters

long-standing and musically complex—and because the musical "language" is shared with other kinds of Chinese music such as opera, narrative songs, and ritual music. [See the sidebar on page 42 for selected recordings of Chinese music.]

Are there forms of children's music within the culture?

There is a small amount of specially composed music for children and teenagers in China today—music for them to sing and play. Children who strive to become more musical typically watch adult performers and imitate their performances at home or in school.

What music do children and teenagers learn in and out of school?

They learn folk songs in singing classes at school, and the talented ones learn the musical instruments of the grown-ups. Children mainly learn specially composed children's songs, many of which are based upon Western major and minor tonalities, though some are in traditional Chinese modes of five and seven tones. [See Chapter 8 of MENC's *Multicultural Perspectives in Music Education* (1989) for examples.] They also learn a few Chinese folk songs, usually with new texts, and a few foreign songs, such as "Twinkle, Twinkle Little Star" and songs by Stephen Foster. Through family and community gatherings, children also learn songs of adult pop-singing stars. Television is the main media, and some families have video and karaoke sets. Western pop music has become available on cassette tapes and CDs in the last ten years and is very popular. (In the countryside, television is less common, so the situation is probably different; in remote areas, children do not even have singing classes in school.) While many teachers and other experts have criticized the practice of having children imitate adults' songs, educational authorities lack effective methods for dealing with the problem.

What might you suggest as introductory experiences in the music of China?

I would suggest that initial experiences focus on the musical sound rather than explanations and cultural

Cantonese narrative singer Du Huan with Bell Yung in a Hong Kong teahouse.

background of the music. For younger children, music can be combined with games and dancing, and music can be played during art classes, lunch, and recess periods. For middle and high school choirs, there is a sizable choral repertory of twentieth-century music from China to be performed. These songs are mainly based upon folk and traditional tunes, but are given a Western common-practice harmonic treatment. Orchestral and band repertory is more problematic, and I cannot think of any easy solution for translating Chinese ensemble music to Western orchestra or band. A bold proposal is to suggest that high schools contract musicians who can teach students Chinese musical instruments. It may be useful to note that some Chinese instruments are not too different from Western ones: erh-hu shares some features with violin, pipa with guitar, sanxian (pronounced "SAHN-shen") with banjo, dixi with flute, and xiao with recorder. Such comparisons could be made, and perhaps some adaptation of Chinese musical pieces by school ensembles could be accomplished.

If teachers and students are performing Chinese music, what elements should be noted and approached with musical and cultural sensitivity?

I would recommend simply that students be taught to respect music of other peoples, whether or not they themselves like it. I would stress that, even though Chinese music may seem strange at first, it is pleasing, beautiful, and exciting to some Chinese children. Similarly, music that American children like may also sound strange to Chinese children at first. I would de-emphasize differences of cultural values in the U.S. and China, and would emphasize what they share: music that is appreciated for its beauty and excitement.

When I was growing up in China and Hong Kong, I was introduced to Western art music through recordings of famous compositions and performers. No one gave me information of the cultural background or context of the music, but by listening I developed a sense of what was "good music" and worth listening to again. An emphasis on the cultural and social background of unfamiliar music tends to alienate the children from the music rather than draw them closer to it. Verbal knowledge about music and its context is less important than the message that the music conveys: that it is beautiful and worthwhile learning. ■

CHRISTOPHER WATERMAN ON YORUBA MUSIC OF AFRICA

This interview with Christopher Waterman focuses on the music of the Yoruba people of Nigeria and, more generally, sub-Saharan Africa.

BY PATRICIA SHEHAN CAMPBELL

The son of two cultural anthropologists, Christopher Waterman may have been born to be one himself. His father, Richard A. Waterman, was a jazz musician and ethnomusicologist with expertise in sub-Saharan African, Afro-Cuban, Caribbean, and Australian aboriginal musics. His mother, Patricia Waterman, a professor of anthropology at the University of South Florida, specializes in Native American, Australian aboriginal, and Irish cultures. From his birth in 1954 to his present position as one of the most dynamic members of a new generation of ethnomusicologists, Christopher Waterman has carried with him an anthropological wisdom instilled early on through his first home-and-family culture.

Waterman's father was a friend of jazz musicians such as Dizzy Gillespie, Al McKebban, and Cannonball Adderley. During their jazz sessions in the basement, young Christopher napped in his crib while tunes trickled up through the air duct beneath him.

Patricia Shehan Campbell is professor in the School of Music at the University of Washington in Seattle and chair of the Society for Ethnomusicology's Education Committee.

Christopher Waterman

Photo by Mary Levin

Various musicians and professors visited the Waterman home throughout his childhood, and Christopher remembers his conversations with a Yoruban professor of history from Nigeria as being particularly provocative when he was the impressionable age of twelve.

Waterman attended public schools in Detroit and Tampa. He began play-

ing string bass at age seven and tuba at age twelve and has been a professional bassist (both string and electric) in jazz and rock groups since the age of fourteen. Driven to continue his interests in jazz at the Berklee College of Music in Boston, he received his bachelor's in composition in 1976. He went on the road with the Macar brothers, winning the first student small-group jazz award from *Downbeat* magazine in 1977. Playing in clubs five or six nights a week, he began to question why it was that people came out to hear popular music, to dance to it, and to play it. He read Alan P. Merriam's *The Anthropology of Music* (Merriam had been a student of his father) and visited with various anthropologists and ethnomusicologists when his band would take him to their towns. Thus, he was drawn into the formal study of ethnomusicology.

Waterman pursued graduate studies in anthropology and music at the University of Illinois, where he received a doctorate in anthropology in 1986. With an avid interest in African American culture and history, he found a prominence of Yoruban terminology and concepts in neo-African religious traditions of the Caribbean and South America. He wondered, "Who were the Yoruba people, anyway?" He conducted field-work in Nigeria, particularly in the cities of Lagos and Ibadan, where he studied the music, musicians, audiences, and culture at large, while playing bass in popular juju bands. Presently associate professor of music and anthropology at the University of Washington in Seattle, Waterman is also chair of the university's African Studies Committee. His undergraduate classes in world-beat and popular music and song draw capacity crowds of 700-plus students, due not only to the subject matter but also to his remarkable teaching style—a rare blend of wit and humor with an interdisciplinary approach to the study of music in culture.

Waterman is author of *Juju: A Social History and Ethnography of an African Popular Music* (University of Chicago Press, 1990), the "Africa" sections of *Ethnomusicology: Historical and Regional Studies* (Norton, 1993), and various articles on African and American music in *Ethnomusicology, Passages,* and assorted essay collections. He also compiled and edited the recording *Juju Roots: 1930s–1950s* (Rounder CD 5017). He was first vice president of the Society for Ethnomusicology (SEM) from 1992 to 1994 and served as coeditor of the SEM newsletter from 1988 to 1991 and council member from 1986 to 1988. His current work includes the analysis of Yoruba music videos; in this analysis, he gives careful attention to the music, visual images, and language, studying how these components work together and what social commentary they provide. He continues to play bass in jazz, rock, and Afro-pop bands and has the callouses to prove it.

Here are Waterman's responses to questions about music of the Yoruba and the world.

How should the study of the world's musical cultures be integrated within the school curriculum?

It is important that students be exposed to a variety of musical styles as early as possible in their education. The standard way for teachers to do this is to prepare units on specific traditions: this week Africa, next week Indonesia, and so on. Depending upon the goals of the teacher, it might also be possible to juxtapose performances from different traditions within a single lesson.

How might different musical traditions be blended into a single lesson?

One might, for example, play and discuss a recording of a piece from the Western art music repertory, perhaps a Beethoven symphony, and then play and discuss a non-Western polyphonic recording, perhaps a "song of rejoicing after a hunt" by the Ba-Benzele people from central Africa (from *Music of the Ba-Benzele Pygmies,* Musicaphon BM 30 L2303). One could show how Beethoven takes a set of elementary musical ideas and develops them. This approach to musical creation is related to a particular conception of "progress" (development, recapitulation, large-scale forms, and the idea of musical "pieces" and "works"). Beethoven is regarded as the sole author of the piece. Conductors and performers attempt to interpret his intentions, and are generally not allowed much latitude to improvise. The overall organization of the ensemble and musical roles is hierarchical, with the conductor at the apex. Although the best conductors and performers commit the music to memory, a

Figure 1. Africa

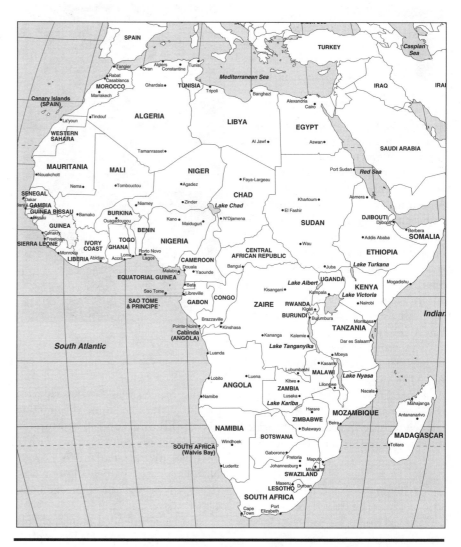

symphony by Beethoven is transmitted primarily in written form.

The Ba-Benzele performance, not a "piece" of music as much as an event, is also based upon a set of simple patterns that, in combination, create a rich polyphonic texture. But, the logic of their combination is very different. One of the most important techniques is hocketing, in which each part, consisting of only a few notes repeated over and over in a cycle, is placed carefully in time so that it interlocks with the other parts. Individuals improvise, but only within fairly strict limits, since varying the constituent parts too much would unravel the overall texture. This texture is an expression of egalitarian social values, in a society in which there are no inherited offices—no chiefs or kings. All of the members of a given community—men, women, and children—participate in making music at such events. The knowledge for producing this kind of music—the individual parts and their rules for combination—is transmitted aurally and must be held in memory by the performers.

These two approaches to developing rich musical textures from simple ideas could provide the basis for a stimulating discussion not only about music itself, but also about its relationship to some basic questions: How do we distinguish "good" music from "bad" music? Is there more than one way for music to be "good" and, if so, why? One might focus on the issue of complexity in music since both pieces generate a great deal of complexity from fairly simple underlying principles. The point is not to put either type of music down, but to stimulate the students to think about what they are hearing. In a Beethoven and Ba-Benzele comparison, the variety of musical concepts and structures in different societies can be emphasized, and students can be encouraged to consider multiple ways of conceptualizing musical creativity and complexity. This kind of juxtaposition can, if done the right way, put Western art music in a broader context, as one among many musics. It may challenge students (and teachers) to rethink certain preconceptions and prejudices.

Can we assume that, due to the popularity of world-beat music, students know more about the world's musical cultures today than they once did?

The popularity of world-beat music—a diverse marketing category that includes African pop, Bulgarian women's choirs, and Sufi devotional music—has increased over the last few years. Nonetheless, the percentage of the American listening public that buys CDs by world-beat stars King Sunny Ade of Nigeria or Nusrat Fateh Ali Khan of Pakistan is relatively minuscule. Even those kids who listen to such music learn very little about the way it is put together or about its cultural context from the skimpy liner notes provided.

■ ■ ■ ■ ■

Individuals improvise, but only within fairly strict limits, since varying the constituent parts too much would unravel the overall texture.

■ ■ ■ ■ ■

I do think that the work of impresario-superstars such as Paul Simon and David Byrne can provide a kind of "bridge" into traditional musics. For example, one could play a song from Simon's 1986 *Graceland* album featuring a Zulu male choir, Ladysmith Black Mambazo (LBM), and then compare it to an example of traditional Zulu polyphonic singing. Most students will probably prefer the LBM example at first, since it more closely approximates what they are

used to hearing in terms of texture and intonation. But, one can point out that certain types of musical complexity are lost in the Westernized example and that the traditional example is interesting in different ways. Of course, students don't have to like everything they hear, but they should learn to think about the bases for their judgments ("I like the first example better because...."). This is one essential aim of education: the development of critical thought.

What suggestions do you have for teachers who wish to pursue the study of musical cultures of the world?

College-level texts, such as *Excursions in World Music* by Bruno Nettl et al. (Prentice-Hall, 1992), can help teachers get a handle on major styles and the uses and meanings of music in various societies. As always, listening to music is an indispensable part of the learning process. Find out which institutions near you (public libraries, universities, or college radio stations) have a collection of world music recordings. And don't be afraid to contact your local ethnomusicologist. The nature of our training and our teaching duties means that we are both specialists and generalists, capable of teaching about our own fieldwork and about a broad array of world musics. The ethnomusicologists I know are glad to do what they can to contribute to the diversification of music education in public and private schools.

What is the musical culture of your own expertise?

My main area of interest is sub-Saharan African musics and cultures. [Editor's note: Ethnomusicologist usually make a distinction between Islamic north Africa and the culturally heterogeneous area below the Sahara desert known as sub-Saharan Africa.] My field research has focused on the music of the Yoruba of southwestern Nigeria, particularly the forms of popular music that have developed in urban centers during the twentieth century.

What is the incidence of this musical culture in the United States?

The dundun, known as the "talking drum," has become a symbol of Yoruba identity.

Photo courtesy of Christopher Waterman

which the relative pitch of syllables helps to determine their meaning. Yoruba, like some other west African languages, has three tonal levels: low, mid, and high. To give one example, the word *bata* spoken on two low tones means a shoe; the word *bata* spoken on a low and then a high tone means a type of drum. The ability to "speak" with the instrument lends depth to Yoruba drumming, a depth not evident to the Western percussionist who merely imitates the surface sound of the instrument. A dundun drummer can praise a wealthy patron in order to extract a gift or verbally abuse a reluctant donor; he can recite a "deep" proverb or cite the latest urban slang; and he can find employment in a wide variety of musical contexts, ranging from sacred possession-trance rituals to the popular dance music performed at parties and nightclubs. The dundun has come to function as a generalized symbol of Yoruba identity and has even been used as an emblem by politicians seeking to mobilize popular support. [Various aspects of dundun drumming and its role in Yoruba society are well-illustrated in Akin Euba's book *Yoruba Drumming: The Dundun Tradition* (Bayreuth University African Studies Series 21/22, 1990).]

How is Yoruba contemporary music the same or different from what it was in the past?

Contrary to stereotypical images of African societies seen in American popular culture, Yoruba society is highly cosmopolitan and dynamic. The Yoruba have lived in large cities for centuries and have complex markets, sophisticated philosophical systems, and a general openness to the incorporation of foreign styles and technologies. The sort of changes that have taken place in syncretic pop styles such as juju music, in which synthesizers may be used to "talk" and multiple electric guitars are arranged in interlocking patterns like drums in a traditional ensemble, are actually quite traditional. [Juju is a form of popular music that originated in Lagos, Nigeria, in the 1920s; it blends Yoruba aesthetics, texts, and talking drums with Western instruments and

There are several hundred thousand Nigerians in the U.S., concentrated in Brooklyn, Chicago, Houston, and other cities. Many of them are Yoruba. Popular Nigerian musicians touring the U.S. often perform specifically for the expatriate Nigerian community. During the World Cup soccer games in the U.S. in 1994, Yoruba musical instruments such as the "talking drum" were used by the enthusiastic rooting section that followed the Nigerian team.

What is the meaning of music to the Yoruba people?

Music is closely bound up with kinship, religion, politics, and economics. It is used to celebrate stages in the human life course, and it is intertwined with other genres of expressive behavior, including dance, visual and plastic arts, and poetic speech. Yoruba music encompasses literally hundreds of named genres and dozens of types of instruments. It ranges from secret performances connected with "deep"

powerful rituals to the public performances of popular music superstars—public performances broadcast on radio and television and sold by bootleg cassette vendors.

Is there a single "most representative" music of the Yoruba?

The musical repertoire that many Yoruba take to be emblematic of their culture is that of the dundun, or talking drum. The dundun is a two-headed drum with an hourglass-shaped wooden body; the two heads are connected by a series of leather thongs that run the length of the drum's body. When these thongs are pulled or squeezed, the tension on the heads is increased, and the fundamental pitch rises. This ability to control pitch allows the drummer to imitate the contours of spoken Yoruba and to articulate various types of poetic speech (proverbs, praises, and so on).

How can the dundun "talk"?

Yoruba is a tonal language, in

technologies.] As one pop bandleader said to me, "Our tradition is a very modern tradition." The study of Yoruba popular music is a good antidote to the stereotypical image of "darkest Africa" as a terrarium for ancient ways of life and to the idea that tradition is synonymous with stasis.

What music do Yoruba children perform?

As in many African societies, there are some repertoires particular to children. However, the style of children's songs is not markedly different from the mainstream of Yoruba music. There are singing games and songs learned at primary school and in church (with Yoruba lyrics and European melodies). Kids also imitate pop music styles, using cardboard boxes, tin cans, pen caps, and other discarded objects. [See C. Waterman, "The Junior Fuji Stars of Agbowo: Popular Music and Yoruba Children," in *Music and Child Development,* edited by F. R. Wilson and F. L. Roehmann (St. Louis: MMB Music, 1990).]

What would you suggest as introductory experiences in Yoruba music for teachers and their students?

Regrettably, there are to my knowledge no readily available recordings of traditional Yoruba music with reasonable sound quality and detailed liner notes. Instead, I would use a selection from a popular music recording, perhaps "Jà Fún Mi" ("Fight for Me") from King Sunny Ade's 1982 *Juju Music* album (Island Records). This example not only illustrates basic principles of Yoruba music and west African music in general, but also helps to dispel stereotypes about Africa and Africans. This music is very traditional in some regards, yet it is played on electronic instruments and incorporates aspects of European and American styles.

In presenting a lesson on "Jà Fún Mi," I would begin with a discussion of aspects of African musical style. Tom Turino's article on African music in *Excursions in World Music* (Prentice-Hall, 1992) is a source of background information. This could be followed by listening to the music several times, with focus on the talking drum, the

Photo courtesy of Christopher Waterman

Dundun drummers are involved in a wide variety of musical contexts, from street music performances, as shown here, to sacred rituals.

leader and chorus, the call-and-response singing, the repetition in the supporting parts, and so forth. Then one could discuss the function of the music: it is party music, it is music for dancing, and it fulfills some of the functions of traditional praise poetry and proverbs. "Jà Fún Mi" is not a romantic "I Love You, Baby" sort of song text; it deals with character, fate, and the dangers of living in a competitive world, as reflected in such lyrics as "Hard world, ultimate world, amazing world/ The world is a whip." I can imagine a variety of projects following the listening and discussion, once students have a chance to experience how all aspects of the song, the rhythm, melody, and song texts, fit together to form a cohesive whole. Students might then be able to compose and perform a song in the style, backed with appropriate rhythmic accompaniment.

Video sequences help to reinforce the music. There is a sequence featuring juju musician Sunny Ade in a

video called *Konkombe,* part of the Beats of the Heart series released in the U.S. by Shanachie Records. Sunny is also featured prominently in "Juju Music," a segment of the National Geographic Explorer series, produced by Jacques Hollander.

What should teachers know about cultural values and behaviors of the Yoruba, Nigerians, and Africans, in general, in order to teach their music with sensitivity?

Nigerians are very proud of the attention that their various cultures (there are more than two hundred distinct languages in this one nation) have received in the U.S. in recent years. They are also often understandably sensitive about portrayals of Africa as a cultural backwater or of Africans as "primitives." It is important to present the music and its cultural context with respect and to combat stereotypes. Contrary to the images portrayed in films and on television, African music is not a wild

Lesson Plan for Features of Yoruba Music

Objectives

Students will:

- perform high, mid, and low tones to represent sounds in the Yoruba tonal language

- perform interlocking rhythmic patterns using percussion instruments

- sing a song that features call-and-response form

Materials

- drums (with three tones: high, mid, and low) or substitute chairs or desks (again, with three tones)

- other assorted drums

Procedures

1. *Talking Drum.* As an illustration of the dundun (talking drum) and its link to the Yoruba language, use a three-toned drum or various classroom objects (such as a chair or desk) to perform high, mid, and low tones. Do the following activities:

- explore the drum or playing object for high, mid, and low tones

- practice performing high and low tones for timbral and rhythmic clarity

- speak the following phrases in the Yoruba singing game "Tolongo," and then "play" them using appropriate high (H), mid (M), and low (L) tones, as marked (if necessary, tell the students that "ocher" and "indigo" are colors):

MM HM LLL MM
Ẹyẹ mélo tolongo ayé
(Ay-yay may-loh toh-lohn-goh ah-yay)
(How many birds are creeping on the earth?)

LM HH MH
Ìkan dúdú áró
(Ee-kahn doo-doo ah-roh)
(One is dark indigo.)

LM LL ML
Ìkan sésé osùn
(Ee-kahn say-say oh-suhn)
(One is bright ocher.)

LM H H M HM HM
Ìkan ṣo-ṣo-ṣo firù bálè
(Ee-kahn soh-soh-soh fee-ruh bah-leh)
(Only one is putting its tail on the ground.)

Yoruba Singing Game

2. *Hocketing*. Using four drums, play the interlocking drum pattern shown below; this is a rhythm for words directed to Òsun, a Yoruba river deity. Note that the top line should be played by a drum that can produce high, mid, and low tones. The second line can feature a high drum and a low drum playing the two parts in a hocketing fashion. The third line can be played by a single drum with high- and low-tone potential and is the same rhythm as the second line. Present the piece, leading to the addition of the sung melody, through the following sequence:

- Chant the top line rhythmically, using the words "low," "mid," and "high." The teacher may play this lead drum part as students "play" on various objects. Eventually, students are charged with this rhythmic pattern on the "talking drum."

- Chant the third line rhythmically, using the words "low" and "high." Play it on various objects, eventually shifting it to drums.

- Chant the second line, noting that it is the same as the third line except that it is played on two drums. Divide students into high and low parts, asking that they "play" either the low or high tones on various objects. Eventually, assign students to low and high

drums on which to play the interlocking tones.

- Sing the melody of the first line. Note that its Yoruba text "Òsun, bá mi sé" (Oh-shuhn bah-mee-shay) translates as "Òsun, help me to do it." The "it" may refer to any physical or mental challenge, from climbing or swimming a river to doing one's homework.

- Layer in the parts, starting with the third pattern, the two supporting drums of the second pattern, the lead drum's first-line pattern, and then the sung melody.

3. *Call-and-Response*. To learn about an important structural element of Yoruba music, sing a traditional song that features call-and-response, such as the Yoruba singing game "Tolongo" (on page 40). Sing it with its solo and group-response parts, with the middle two phrases (measures 2 and 3) sung four times. Once the song is learned, younger children can play the game: (a) form a circle, (b) step steadily on the beat, to the right, and (c) on the last phrase, sit down (putting bird tails on the ground). For older children, sing the song while playing the high, mid, and low tones of the song's lyrics on drums (see text on page 40 for the H, M, and L markings on the words).

Rhythm for Òṣun

Transcription by Christopher Waterman

outpouring of unbridled emotion, but rather is music fundamentally concerned with principles like restraint, balance, and sharing. For example, if one person plays his or her part too loudly or improvises inappropriately, he or she ruins the music for everyone.

■ ■ ■ ■ ■ ■

Sudents don't even have a shot at imitation unless they've had a chance to hear an unfamiliar musical style, a distinctive vocal timbre, or a rhythmic "feel."

■ ■ ■ ■ ■ ■

Is the authenticity of a musical performance an issue in Yoruba culture? Should it be for music teachers and their students?

Among the Yoruba of Nigeria, the operative term is *ijinle,* literally "deep in the earth." People sometimes argue about which performers or types of music are really "deep Yoruba," "authentic," and "traditional" and which are not. For music teachers, the issue is an important one as well. Does a given choral arrangement of a Yoruba song bear any relationship to traditional Yoruba singing, or is it simply another "grind-'em-out" SATB arrangement incorporating a vaguely African melody? In my high school stage band class, it always bothered me that we never set aside class time to listen to recordings of the Count Basie arrangements we were trying to play. Most of the students, largely middle-class white

kids, were being asked to play a kind of music they hadn't heard and to swing without the chance to develop an aural model of swinging. The point is not to create a "perfect" imitation of Kansas City jazz, Korean singing, or west African drumming (it's hard to know what a "perfect" imitation would be, anyway). But, students don't even have a shot at imitation unless they've had a chance to hear an unfamiliar musical style, a distinctive vocal timbre, or a rhythmic "feel." The combination of informed listening (hearing a style and thinking about how it's put together) with mimesis (learning through imitation) is a powerful one. These techniques should complement one another.

Can you recommend further sources for teaching the music of African peoples?

Let Your Voice Be Heard: Songs from Ghana and Zimbabwe (World Music Press, 1986), arranged and annotated by Abraham Kobena Adzinyah, Dumisani Maraire, and Judith Cook Tucker, is an excellent source for K–12 teachers. It includes transcriptions and a cassette. Sources such as David Locke's *Drum Gahu: A Systematic Method for an African Percussion Piece* (While Cliffs Media, 1987) and Peter Cooke's *Play Amadinda: Xylophone Music of Uganda* (K & C Productions of Edinburgh, 1990) include detailed performance instructions and accompanying cassettes. Cooke's pamphlet also includes instructions for making a simple xylophone.

There are a variety of useful publications on the music of the Shona people of Zimbabwe, including Paul Berliner's *The Soul of Mbira* (University of California Press, 1978), which is keyed to Nonesuch recordings and includes instructions on making the instrument, and Claire Jones's *Making Music: Musical Instruments of Zimbabwe Past and Present* (Academic Books, 1992). The best guides to the literature on African music are John Gray's *African Music: A Bibliographical Guide to the Traditional, Popular, Art and Liturgical Musics of Sub-Saharan Africa* (Greenwood Press, 1991) and Carol Lems-Dworkin's *African Music: A Pan-African Annotated Bibliography* (Hans Zell, 1991). ■

Objectives

Students will:

- discuss and identify features in African music that are found within Yoruba juju music

- discuss the meaning of the lyrics to "Jà Fún Mi"

- perform components of "Jà Fún Mi" vocally and on various instruments

- compose a new song in a similar style

Materials

- "Jà Fún Mi" recording, from *King Sunny Ade: Juju Music* (Island Records ILPS 9712)

- drums

- cowbell

- bass guitar

Procedures

1. Discuss aspects of African musical style: call-and-response singing, interlocking patterns sung or played instrumentally, dense textures, the delicate balance between repetition and improvisation, and the importance of rhythmic flow (the "groove").

2. Review procedures from the other lesson plan on the talking drum, interlocking parts, and call-and-response structure.

3. Listen to "Jà Fún Mi." Pay particular attention to the talking drum (a low swooping sound), the leader and chorus, the call-and-

Lesson Plan for "Jà Fún Mi"

by Patricia Shehan Campbell and Christopher Waterman

response singing, the repetition in the supporting parts, and the improvisation in the performance of the lead singer and lead guitarist. Note the way in which all the parts intertwine to form a densely woven texture, somewhat like the threads of a tapestry, and "feel" the gentle but powerful rhythmic momentum.

4. Discuss the function of the music: party music, music for dancing, and music that fulfills some of the functions of traditional praise poetry and proverbs.

5. Read and discuss the text. The lyrics are closer to the hard-core realism of rap music or alternative groups such as Nirvana and Pearl Jam than to mainstream American pop. Here is a portion of the translation (note that the "Blue Touraco" is a parrot and that "one's head" means "one's destiny"):

My head, please, fight for me, my spirit, please, fight, fight for me
My head, please, fight for me, my spirit, please, fight, fight for me
Because the Blue Touraco's head fights for the Blue Touraco, the head of the Aluko bird fights, oh
Because the Blue Touraco's head fights for the Blue Touraco, the head of the Aluko bird fights, oh
My Creator, don't forget me, it is better that you fight, oh

Hard world, ultimate world, amazing world, world
The world is a whip, if it swings forward, then it swings backward in return
The world is a whip, if it swings forward, then it swings backward in return
One's head brings good luck to one
Head, let me land in a good place
Legs, lead me to a good place
Head, let me land in a good place
Legs, lead me to a good place
Because, each person must be responsible for his own affairs
Because, each person must be responsible for his own affairs*

6. Perform components of "Jà Fún Mi," without the recording as well as with it. Use the notation shown below for the first line of the song, pronounced "Oh-ree mee yay, jah, jah fuhn mee, ay-dah mee yay-oh."

7. Compose a new song in the style of "Jà Fún Mi," Sunny Ade, and modern juju music.

*Source of text: Christopher Waterman, *Juju Music,* © by the University of Chicago Press, 1991. Used by permission. See pages 142–44 for the complete Yoruba text and English translation.

Excerpt from "Jà Fún Mi"

Transcription by Patricia Shehan Campbell

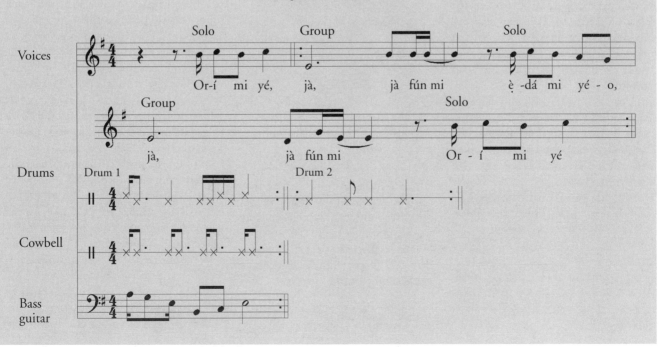

MELLONEE BURNIM ON AFRICAN AMERICAN MUSIC

As part of the "Music in Cultural Context" series, this interview with Mellonee Burnim focuses on the gospel music of African Americans.

BY PATRICIA SHEHAN CAMPBELL

Until her senior year of high school, Mellonee Burnim attended all-Black schools and churches in rural Teague, Texas. The all-Black Methodist and Baptist churches of her hometown provided her with firsthand knowledge of the music that was to become an important part of her life's work. She was singing gospel music in elementary school and, by the age of twelve, was pianist for three choirs in the three churches. Because Black-based sacred music was "in the air" of her African American community, she learned by ear its essence and power and her own musicianship was firmly established from her childhood onward.

Burnim enrolled in North Texas State University as a music education major, with a piano concentration and a secondary emphasis in voice. There she studied classical repertoire and technique, while on Sundays she would play piano for services in a small Black Baptist church some thirty miles away. She was utilizing the

---

Patricia Shehan Campbell is professor in the School of Music at the University of Washington in Seattle and chair of the Society for Ethnomusicology's Education Committee.

Mellonee Burnim

Photo courtesy of Mellonee Burnim

bimusicality—Western European and African American—that had developed during her childhood. On graduation, she accepted a middle school choral position in Texas, where she taught sixth-grade general music and directed three seventh- and eighth-grade choirs. Burnim recalls:

My classroom was the auditorium, if you can imagine.

When I went there, not one choir had a single male in it, and also there was not a single African American student enrolled in the choral program. … I knew I had to reach the students where they were musically … so I had to explore musics beyond my formal training. … The challenge led me to pursue further study of a greater variety of music.

Burnim concentrated her studies in African music at the master's level, writing a thesis at the University of Wisconsin–Madison on songs in Mende (Liberian) folktales. In 1980, she completed a doctorate in ethnomusicology through the Department of Folklore at Indiana University. Her research, then and now, on the Black gospel music tradition as a symbol of ethnicity, reflects the duality of her training in both African and African American music. She has published articles on gospel music in *Ethnomusicology* and *Music Educators Journal* and has contributed essays to such collections as *More than Dancing: Essays on Afro-American Music and Musicians* (1985), *Expressively Black* (1987), and *African American Religion* (1992). Currently, she is completing manuscripts on African American religious

Thomas A. Dorsey (1899–1993) was a leader of the gospel movement.

sented not through mere geographical overviews of music, but through the juxtaposition of musical examples from various cultures to illustrate music's similarities and differences. This approach to teacher preparation can then be taken by teachers into their own respective teaching assignments.

What is the musical culture of your expertise?

My training is in both African and African American music. My research focuses largely on African American religious music, particularly on gospel music. I also do comparative research, seeking to discover relationships between religious musics in Christian settings among Africans on the continent and among African Americans in the U.S.

What is the meaning and function of gospel music to African Americans?

Gospel music is a celebration and an affirmation of life. It is through the performance of gospel music that African Americans can identify with their cultural and historical past, transcend that past, and achieve the courage and strength to move forward into the future. Gospel music functions in ways similar to the Negro spiritual that was created during the period of slavery; in fact, it is an extension of the spiritual. As part of a musical continuum, gospel music evolved in the early decades of the twentieth century after the great migration of Blacks from the rural South into urban areas of both the North and South. It was first associated with small storefront churches in cities like Chicago, and during its infancy in the early 1930s, gospel pioneers fought to gain acceptance. Today, it is one of the most prominent African American genres, serving as a vital dimension of worship in African American churches across the nation. [See the Resources sidebar for books and recordings recommended by Burnim for the study of African American music and culture.]

How is gospel music related to other African American musical forms?

African American music is a very complex mosaic, and each genre has

music for the much anticipated *Garland Encyclopedia of World Music.*

In addition to scholarly projects, Burnim maintains her strong involvement in gospel music as a performer, teacher, and clinician. As minister of music at Bethel A.M.E. (African Methodist Episcopal) church in Bloomington, Indiana, she plays piano and conducts the choir for Sunday services. She conducts workshops on spirituals and gospel music in the U.S., Cuba, and Malawi (in southeastern Africa), where she brings singers and teachers of various cultural backgrounds into the African American experience.

Here are Burnim's answers to questions about African American music and music in general.

When, where, and why should world musics be taught?

I'm a firm believer that world musics should be taught at all stages of the musical curriculum for students of all ages and cultural backgrounds. Musics of non-European cultures should be taught not only in elementary music classrooms, but also as part of the repertoire of secondary school

choirs, bands, and orchestras. This can be done by teaching incrementally, that is, by adding more complex principles at various stages of learning—just as we do in teaching Western European art music. If children are taught something of the aesthetics *and* mechanics of folk traditions in elementary school, when they reach secondary school they will have the foundation for accurately and sensitively interpreting a broad range of musics.

How can a teacher's training lead to the presentation of a broader musical repertoire to students in elementary and secondary schools?

In the music major degree, some departures will need to be taken from the more traditional repertoire that comprises academic and performance classes. It takes years of study to become skilled in Western European art music, and that same degree of commitment is involved in learning other musical traditions. A teacher's knowledge of specific musical cultures will be well formulated when the musical scope of his or her required undergraduate course work is broadened. Musical diversity must be pre-

mutually influenced the next. The forms are not isolated, but are fit neatly into a unified cultural whole. Jazz cannot be wholly separated from gospel, and blues cannot be altogether separated from the spiritual. From the emergence of the folk spiritual of the late 1700s, with its strong connections both to Western European and West African musical styles, African American music has been a continuum of characteristics that are identifiably "Black." These include call-and-response structures, syncopated rhythms, polyrhythms, blues notes, and the presence of a unique African-derived approach to music making.

What is the representation of African American gospel music in the U.S.?

Gospel music is a pervasive presence in American society today. It is virtually everywhere, particularly since the media has made it available to a vast audience. The "Bobby Jones Gospel Show" on Sunday morning is the number one program on Black Entertainment Television; it is broadcast not only in the U.S. but also in Africa, England, and the Caribbean. Gospel artists can be seen on national television as well, from the Sounds of Blackness on the "Today Show" to Vanessa Bell Armstrong on the "Oprah Winfrey Show." Live performances of gospel music can be heard in Black churches across denominational lines—Pentecostal, Methodist, Baptist, Catholic, Presbyterian, and Lutheran. Gospel is also present on college campuses—every Black college and major university across the nation has at least one gospel choir.

Can you name a "most representative" substyle, composer, performer, or piece of gospel music?

Traditional gospel music is still the major force—it involves choirs, quartets, and solo voices accompanied by instruments ranging from piano or organ alone to a rhythm section of drums, bass, and lead guitars as well as synthesizers and horns. Mahalia Jackson and the Roberta Martin Singers are good examples of pioneers in traditional gospel sound. There is also contemporary gospel, with artists like Tramaine Hawkins, Donald Vails,

Lesson Plan: From Spirituals to Gospel

Objectives

Students will:

- understand through analytical listening and discussion the historical relationship of spirituals and gospel songs

- compare the spiritual "Steal Away to Jesus" to the gospel song "Steal Away"

- compare the spiritual "O Mary, Don't You Weep, Don't You Mourn" to the gospel song "Mary, Don't You Weep"

Materials

- "Steal Away to Jesus" from *Religious Folk Songs of the Negro* (Hampton, VA: Hampton Institute Press, 1927)

- "Steal Away to Jesus" from *Wade in the Water: African American Sacred Music Traditions* (audiotape set from Smithsonian Institution, 1994)

- "Steal Away," gospel arrangement of chorus, by Phyllis Byrdwell (given with lesson plan)

- "O Mary, Don't You Weep, Don't You Mourn" from *American Negro Songs* (New York: Howell, Soskin & Co., 1940)

- "Mary, Don't You Weep," recorded by the Swan Silvertones on *Jubilation!* (Volume 1: Black Gospel/Rhino Records R2 70288)

- "Mary, Don't You Weep," recorded on *Take Six* (Reprise 9256702)

Procedures

1. Define spiritual as a Black religious song created during the period of slavery and expressive of a range of emotions encompassing joy, hope, and sorrow. By the end of the seventeenth century, African melodies, rhythms, and vocal styles were already fusing with European melodies and texts about Christian concepts of faith, love, and salvation cast through references to Biblical events. The spiritual was brought to the broad attention of American society in the late nineteenth century through the extensive concert tours of the Fisk Jubilee Singers and through the arrangements by Harry Thacker Burleigh (1866–1949) of spirituals as solo art songs for the concert stage. Examples of spirituals include "Swing Low, Sweet Chariot," "Good News," "Every Time I Feel the Spirit," "Nobody Knows the Trouble I've Seen," and "Go Down, Moses."

2. Define gospel as post–World War I Black religious song rooted in spirituals and hymns, but fused with blues, jazz, and other contemporary popular music elements. The first published Black gospel songs were those written by the Reverend C. Albert Tindley from 1899 to 1906, but the person who exerted the greatest influence on the gospel tradition from the 1920s onward was Thomas A. Dorsey of Chicago. A piano player and ex-bluesman, Dorsey emphasized the beat, added blues riffs, and gave maximum latitude to the soloist and accompanists for improvisation. Gospel music features drums, guitars, and piano or organ, often in the popular style of the day—from blues and jazz to rhythm and blues and rap. Songs like "Precious Lord," "Move On Up a Little Higher," "By and By," "Pre-

cious Memories," and "Oh Happy Day" were recorded by such gospel artists as Mahalia Jackson, Aretha Franklin, Reverend James Cleveland, the Staple Singers, and the Edwin Hawkins Singers.

3. Sing or play the spiritual "Steal Away to Jesus." Note that the historical manuscript was edited by composer R. Nathaniel Dett in 1927 for a collection of popular "Negro" religious songs of the day performed by singers at Hampton Institute, a historically Black college. Call attention to the fact that despite the indications of tempo and dynamic shadings, the notated spiritual (particularly the solo section) is in fact given greater expression than can be indicated. Discuss the presence of solo and choral sections, syncopated rhythms, four-part harmony, and the Christian text suggestive of the singer's return to the Lord for salvation ("stealing away" from the human to the spiritual world).

4. Sing or play the gospel arrangement of the chorus of "Steal Away" (shown below). Note that the melody is vaguely reminiscent of the spiritual, but that the harmonies are a leap from the more traditional progressions found in the spiritual version. This is the chorus section only, which provides group unity and stability in its precision of performance and contrasts dramatically with the solo improvisations. Phyllis Byrdwell, Seattle-based gospel choir director and middle school teacher, arranged the piece for her choristers and students.

5. Sing or play the spiritual "O Mary, Don't You Weep, Don't You Mourn." In the 1940 collection of American Negro religious and secular folk songs, solo and chorus sections are interspersed in relaying Christian beliefs and Biblical characters. "Mary" is the sorrowful mother of Jesus, and the reference to "Pharaoh" and his army from Egypt reminds the listener of the Old Testament story of the legions of soldiers in pursuit of Moses. The seas were parted for Moses' escape, but drawn back to their original state, drowning the soldiers. The verses tell of great longing for salvation in heaven. Double entendre is vital; the story of deliverance symbolizes hope for an enslaved people.

6. Play recordings of two gospel arrangements of "Mary, Don't You Weep," noting at the outset that little remains of the spiritual beyond the text of the chorus section. The first is performed by the Swan Silvertones, a male gospel quartet (a subgenre of gospel with its own dinstinctive traits). Recorded in 1959, the style is distinctly influenced by the rhythm-and-blues style popular at that time. Listen for the interplay of vocal solo and group response and for the instrumental ensemble of acoustic guitar, string bass, and drum. Also typical of gospel quartet music of this period is the I-IV-V vocal and instrumental progression and, of course, hand clapping. Compare this earlier version with the sound of Take Six, a contemporary gospel ensemble. Ask: "How is the Take Six gospel performance clearly more contemporary than the Swan Silvertones performance?" (The technology is more advanced, and the vocal and rhythmic nuances are distinctively different.)

Steal Away

"Steal Away" arrangement, © 1982 by Phyllis Byrdwell. Used by permission.

Albertina Walker, and John P. Kee. Gospel music is continually evolving and is influenced by popular music of the time. A contemporary gospel group like A-1 Swift blends rap elements into their sound in an attempt to reach the youth market. Gospel is not static music, so a "most representative" style is not easy to name.

■ ■ ■ ■ ■ ■

Gospel music is a celebration and an affirmation of life.

■ ■ ■ ■ ■ ■

Is gospel music connected in any way to other African American performing arts?

Absolutely. Gospel music incorporates and embodies a principle that I define as the integration of song and dance. When one sings gospel music, one sings it completely and totally, immersed in body and in spirit. When members of a gospel choir enter the sanctuary for morning worship, they process while clapping their hands and moving their feet in synchrony. Once in the choir box, choir members move following the instructions of their director.

This music-and-movement connection can be traced to many African American musical traditions, ranging from the eighteenth-century "ring shout," a specific style of singing a folk spiritual, when members of the group formed a circle and moved in a counter-clockwise motion, to half-time shows performed by Black marching bands. African American music, and most certainly gospel, is too powerful not to involve the body in synchronous movement.

How early do children learn gospel music in the Black churches? In what ways?

Children sing gospel music from the time they're old enough to feel secure singing. Most Black churches have children's choirs and also youth groups for middle and high school students. They learn early on that gospel music is a means of worship, and they learn to perform it through their own active engagement in the worship service.

What suggestions do you have for teachers and their students who wish to learn gospel music?

Gospel music must be learned and experienced in its context. It cannot be learned by reading musical notation or by studying the score in isolation from the musical performance. Listening to recordings is a valuable and important experience, but a vital element of the live performance is the performer-audience interplay. There's nothing like being at an actual church service where you hear and see what the congregation is responding to, and you note the level of energy that is generated and exchanged by performers and their audience. Recordings often contain abbreviated performances, when, in fact, some of the most creative things in a gospel performance occur at the end of a song—during a vamp section or a reprise. I'd recommend joining a community choir or at least attending rehearsals of a reputable local gospel group. Black churches are wonderful contexts for learning, where people of any culture, age, or religious background are warmly welcomed. There are also conventions and workshops: the National Convention of Gospel Choirs and Choruses, which was founded in the 1930s, and the James Cleveland Gospel Music Workshop of America. These and other workshops are announced in a magazine called *Gospel Today* (originally called *Score*).

What musico-aesthetic matters should be kept in mind in the performance of gospel music?

The performance of music of any culture must be done within the aesthetic framework of the culture in question. This is not to assume that

Objectives

Students will:

■ listen to and analyze a live performance of a gospel song

■ learn to sing a gospel song as a choir

■ experiment with singing solos within the gospel music aesthetic

Materials

■ "Till We Meet Again" from the recording *Kirk Franklin and the Family* (GCD2119, GospoCentric, Inc., 417 E. Regent St., Inglewood, CA 90301; 310-677-5603)

■ Piano

■ Notation/Guide (given with the lesson plan)

Procedures

1. Explain that while gospel music has been developing since the early part of the twentieth century, the emergence of gospel choirs interspersed with solo singers is a slightly more recent phenomenon. With James Cleveland's founding of the Gospel Music Workshop of America in 1968, mass and community choirs sprang up around the nation. Among these are the Florida Mass Choir, the Southern California Community Choir, Edwin Hawkins' Love Center Choir, and the Minnesota-based Sounds of Blackness. These large choirs are known for their split-second timing, pyrotechnic solo improvisations, and shouts and interjections by members of their audience.

2. Listen to the first verse of Kirk Franklin's "Till We Meet Again." Direct students' attention to the choir and piano accompaniment. Ask: "Do the singers perform in unison or harmony?" (Mostly in unison, with two phrases in harmony.)

Lesson Plan for Performing a Gospel Song
by Patricia Shehan Campbell

3. Listen again to the first verse. Pay special attention to the sounds beyond the choir and piano: the words of the choir director and the shouts and claps of the audience. Ask: "What words can you hear from the director and audience?" (Director: "Thank you." "We just want to thank God for what He's done." "Family." "May His peace…" Audience: "Yeah," "Come on," "Ooh," "That's right.") Discuss the performer-audience interplay.

4. Listen for the nuances of the choir voices as they swoop, slur, slide, and glide *together* from one pitch to the next. These ornamental melodic devices are an important characteristic of gospel style. The Notation/Guide (shown below) indicates that the greatest portion of portamenti occurs between adjacent pitches.

5. Sing the melody softly to the recording. While the Notation/Guide may be followed, encourage students to follow as closely as possible the recorded sound of Kirk Franklin's Family singing style, including pronunciations, portamenti, silences, and dynamic shadings. Repeat, striving for unity with the recorded sound. (Note that the two phrases indicated in the notation can be harmonized by an advanced choir, closely following the chord progressions.)

6. Listen to the three solos that follow the choir's verse. Ask: "While the words and melody of the soloists are nearly the same as the choir's verse, how are their versions different from the choir?" (There is much individual freedom in their improvised solos: stretching, sustaining, or rushing the rhythm; jumping the melody a fifth or octave higher or lower; adding trills, passing tones, and portamenti; and varying vocal timbres, from head to chest tones.) Listen again to the solos, focusing on the rhythmic and melodic embellishments discussed.

7. Demonstrate to students how some of these embellishments can be used in improvisatory ways in solo singing. For instance, sing isolated phrases, adding passing tones and trills to the notated melody, particularly on sustained notes at phrase endings and during rests. See the musical examples below for ways to embellish the first five measures. Encourage students to sing these examples and then have them work in small groups to create embellished phrases. Compare their embellishments to those on the recording.

8. As a group, sing the melody with the recording. Ask for volunteers to sing improvised solos, concluding with the full choir.

Till We Meet Again

Codes:

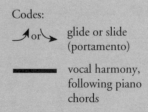

glide or slide (portamento)

vocal harmony, following piano chords

Transcription by Patricia Shehan Campbell. Words and music by Kirk Franklin as recorded by GospoCentric, Inc. © 1993 by Lilly Mack Publishing. All rights reserved. International copyright secured. Used by permission.

Selected Resources

Black History and Culture

Harding, Vincent. *There Is a River: The Black Struggle for Freedom in America.* New York: Vantage, 1983.

Levine, Lawrence. *Black Culture and Black Consciousness.* New York: Oxford, 1978.

Stuckey, Sterling. *Slave Culture: Nationalist Theory and the Foundations of Black America.* New York: Oxford, 1987.

Negro Spirituals

Epstein, Dena. *Sinful Tunes and Spirituals.* Chicago: University of Illinois, 1977.

Southern, Eileen. *The Music of Black Americans: A History.* 2d ed. New York: W. W. Norton, 1983.

Southern, Eileen, ed. *Readings in Black American Music.* 2d ed. New York: W. W. Norton, 1983.

Gospel Music

Burnim, Mellonee. "The Black Gospel Music Tradition: A Complex of Ideology, Aesthetic, and Behavior." In *More than Dancing: Essays on Afro-American Music and Musicians,* edited by Irene Jackson Brown, 147–167. Westport, CT: Greenwood, 1985.

Burnim, Mellonee (with Portia Maultsby). "From Backwoods to City Streets: The Afro-American Musical Journey." In *Expressively Black,* edited by Geneva Gaye and Willie Baber, 109–126. New York: Praeger, 1987.

Harris, Michael. *The Rise of Gospel Blues: The Music of Thomas Andrew Dorsey in the Urban Church.* New York: Oxford, 1992.

Reagon, Bernice Johnson, ed. *We'll Understand It Better By and By.* Washington, DC: Smithsonian Institution Press, 1992.

Recordings: Spirituals

Afro-American Spirituals, Work Songs, and Ballads. Edited by Alan Lomax. Archive of Folk Songs, Library of Congress, AFS L3.

Spirituals. Marian Anderson. RCA AVMI-1735.

Spirituals. Tuskeegee Institute Choir, William Dawson, Director. ABC/Dunhill Records, Westminster Gold WGM 8154.

Recordings: Gospel Music

21 Greatest Hits. Mahalia Jackson. Kenwood 20510.

Africa to America: The Journey of the Drum. Sounds of Blackness. Perspective Records 314549006.

Amazing Grace. Aretha Franklin (with James Cleveland). Atlantic SD 2906.

The Best of the Roberta Martin Singers. The Roberta Martin Singers. Savoy SGL 7018.

Kirk Franklin and the Family. Kirk Franklin. GospoCentric GCS2119.

Love Alive. Walter Hawkins and the Love Center Choir. Light 37760.

Peace Be Still. Vanessa Bell Armstrong. Onyx International Records R3831.

The Promise. James Cleveland and the Philadelphia Mass Choir. Savoy SL 14526.

Wade in the Water: African American Sacred Traditions (four cassette tapes with educator's guide). Smithsonian Institution, 1994.

What a Wonderful Savior I've Found. Donald Vails. Savoy 7025.

You Brought the Sunshine. The Clark Sisters. Sound of Gospel 132.

Gospel choirs use techniques such as call-and-response, staggered entrances, and portamenti.

church services in Mississippi and music at picnics and blues clubs. A good survey of African American musical styles, *Music as Metaphor* (Lawrence Productions, 1988), shows the connections between all forms of performance in the African American community, ranging from jazz to gospel to "art" songs. A source for understanding the tradition of gospel music, *Say Amen, Somebody* (George T. Nierenberg Productions, 1983) chronicles the history of Thomas A. Dorsey, Willie Mae Ford Smith, and Sally Martin—all pioneers in the development of the style. Finally, I would recommend *Saturday Night, Sunday Morning* (Co-Media Productions, 1992), a video about the travels of famous bluesman A. D. "Gatemouth" Moore who, in the middle of his career, had a conversion experience and became a minister and gospel singer. This film documents his involvement on Beale Street in Memphis, the recognition given him by other blues greats like B. B. King (who appears in the film), and his transformation from bluesman to a gospel-singing preacher.

musicians outside the culture will be able to perform gospel with the degree of precision or freedom that characterizes African American performers, but it is essential to strive for the same degree of excellence as we would desire for a performance of Western European music. The energy and joy of gospel music is critical to the sound quality, and this is created only when performers are well rehearsed, relaxed, and confident enough to be wholly engaged in the performance. High school students who are still worrying about notes will give a stilted and mechanical performance. Their teacher must be very comfortable with the rhythms and polyrhythms of a piece as well as the mechanics of staggered entrances, bends, elongated tones, and the shifting of time until students are free of any tentativeness.

Is there a repertoire that young musicians can perform as a step toward African American gospel music?

A good way to build musicianship vital to dealing with all of the aesthetic complexities of gospel music is to have a choral group sing arranged spirituals. This is a notated repertoire, yet some of the same melodic and rhythmic qualities of gospel music are evident in a concert arrangement of spirituals. I would highly recommend arrangements by African American composers (such as Harry Thacker Burleigh, William Dawson, R.

Nathaniel Dett, and Undine Smith Moore) because of their particular adeptness at conveying and translating onto paper the poignant qualities that represent the distinct characteristics of African American music.

What should students in American schools know about gospel music?

Minimally, students should know the names of composers such as Thomas A. Dorsey, Charles A. Tindley, and Doris Akers and performers such as Mahalia Jackson, the Caravans, the Roberta Martin Singers, and James Cleveland. They should understand something of the history of African American religious music and its role and importance in the lives of African Americans. Musically, they should be able to identify a gospel quartet from a gospel choir and should understand something of the characteristics and concepts that comprise it.

Can you recommend resources that can be used to convey an understanding of African American music as a historical phenomenon and a cultural "event"?

I can recommend four videotapes. *The Land Where the Blues Began* (Mississippi Educational TV, 1979) is an excellent film for showing sacred and secular synchrony among different musical genres in African American culture. It includes music from rural

Do you have any closing words regarding the teaching of African American—and world—music in school music programs?

It's a time for seriously rethinking and restructuring music teacher education programs. Teachers cannot teach music they have not been taught, and traditions like gospel music are not learned through a Saturday session or a two-hour, in-service workshop. The musical canon that is delivered to prospective teachers in undergraduate music programs must be rethought, and courses must be designed to give them an understanding of the musical contributions of all Americans—along with the impact of these musics on American society at large. It's a tragedy to hear educated students ask, "Why have we not been told about Marian Anderson and Mahalia Jackson?" I encourage teachers and teacher-educators to take up the challenge, to be of good courage, and to offer their students a musical palette that genuinely reflects the cultural diversity that has made this nation great. ∎

STEVEN LOZA ON LATINO MUSIC

This interview with Steven Loza focuses on the Latino music of Mexico and the Caribbean.

BY PATRICIA SHEHAN CAMPBELL

In the dedication of his book *Barrio Rhythm: Mexican American Music in Los Angeles* (1993), Steven Loza pays tribute to "mis padres, mi profesor, un colega, y los musicos" ("my parents, my professor, a colleague, and the musicians [with whom he has worked]"). Loza himself is a musician, scholar, and teacher who refers to himself as "a homeboy, a sibling" in the great family of Mexican musicians living in Los Angeles. He continues to perform and teach the musical cultures of Chicanos (Mexican Americans), Caribbean peoples, and Latin Americans at large, flavoring the jazz sound of the "Steve Loza Sextet" with these styles.

Loza grew up in the territory of his research; he knows firsthand the musical culture of Mexican Americans in Los Angeles. Throughout his childhood, at home, church, and in the community, he heard "all kinds of Mexican music—*corridos revolucionarios* [revolutionary ballads], Javier Soli, Alberto Vasquez, Rocio Durcal, Vicente Fernandez, Jorge Negrete." He

Patricia Shehan Campbell is professor in the School of Music at the University of Washington in Seattle and chair of the Society for Ethnomusicology's Education Committee.

Steven Loza

Photo courtesy of Steven Loza

began to play trumpet at the age of twelve in an east side archdiocesan youth band in Los Angeles. This led to a jazz scholarship at California State Polytechnic University in Pomona, where he received a bachelor's degree in 1975. His teaching experience began as an assistant band director at Salesian High School, later as a teaching assistant in the band program at Chaffey High School, and then as

band director at St. John Bosco High School (all in the Los Angeles area). For five years (1979–84), he was the lead teacher and program coordinator in migrant education for the state of California, teaching both music and history in high school bilingual education programs.

Loza is currently an associate professor of ethnomusicology at the University of California at Los Angeles, where he completed his master's degree in Latin American studies in 1979 and his doctorate in music in 1985. His academic achievements include both Fulbright and Ford Foundation fellowships and numerous publications in both scholarly and popular press on the topics of Mexican and Latin American music. In his much acclaimed *Barrio Rhythm,* he documents the musical life of Mexican Americans in east Los Angeles from 1945 to the present. Loza edited *Selected Reports in Ethnomusicology: Musical Aesthetics in Los Angeles* (1994), which includes his incisive discussion of music and musicians in one of the most culturally diverse American urban sites. He has served for many years as a member of the Grammy Awards national screening committee and has performed or conducted extensive interviews with such

Latino Musical Styles

Banda [BAHN-dah]: a fusion of *norteño* style with the brass and percussion bands of village fiestas; *bandas* play *norteño* polkas, *ranchera* ballads, and dance music.

Huapango [hooah-PAHN-go]: found in the central Bajío region and along the Gulf coast of eastern Mexico, this instrumental music is played on guitar, *jarana* (small guitar), violin, and sometimes percussion (Ritchie Valens's "La bamba" is a well-known *huapango* number).

Jarocho [ha-RO-ko]: a traditional ensemble in Veracruz (eastern Mexico) that features *requinto* (small guitar-like lute), *jarana,* and harp; associated with music of the Caribbean, especially coastal Venezuela.

Mariachi [ma-ree-AH-chee]: an instrumental ensemble centered in the state of Jalisco, consisting of violins, the vihuela or other guitars, the *guitarrón* (bass guitar), and trumpets.

Norteño [nor-TAYN-yo]: a guitar and accordion ensemble rooted in *corrido* ballads; its lyrics are real stories of heroes and antiheroes (*norteño* music is called "Tex Mex" north of the border).

Ranchera [rahn-CHAY-rah]: mostly nostalgic and pessimistic laments of past times and places; an urban song phenomenon replete with "ay ay ay ay ay" and sustained final tones that end with a glissando.

Son [SOHN]: instrumental music with singing, associated with dance; typically in six beats that are variously accented as two three's or three two's; the plural is *sones* [SOHN-ays].

Salsa [SAHL-sah]: a saucy overhaul of the classic Cuban big-band jazz arrangements, born in the Latin barrios of New York.

Tropical [trop-ee-KAHL]: dance music, including salsa, merengue, *cumbia,* and rumba, played by ensembles of jazz and Afro-Caribbean percussion instruments.

Note: Sources for this information include Gerard Béhague, "Music of Latin America," in Bruno Nettl, *Folk and Traditional Music of the Western Continents* (Englewood Cliffs, NJ: Prentice-Hall, 1994); Peter Manuel, *Popular Musics of the Non-Western World* (New York: Oxford University Press, 1988); and *World Music: The Rough Guide* (London: Rough Guides Ltd., 1994).

Latin musicians as Eddie Cano, Nati Cano, Lalo Guerrero, Tito Puente, Irma Rangel, Linda Ronstadt, Cesar Rosas, Pancho Sanchez, and members of the "Los Illegals" and "Los Lobos" bands.

As a native ethnographer, Loza studies his own musical culture. Even now, between teaching, performance, and research, he returns to his first culture and his family in a Chicano-populated Los Angeles neighborhood. As he tells it:

> I go home and I get fed ... not just food, but life. ... I go home and my dad's listening to Mexican music. ... It's his music and his reality. ... *Arroz con pollo, carne asada,* Sunday's Mass, my mother's rightful nagging, and my father's explosions. ... Reflection.

Here are Loza's answers to questions about Latino music and music in general.

Why should we teach the world's musical cultures?

We owe it to ourselves to be multicultural in the musical education of young people. That means facing the reality of our multicultural American society and making use of technology and travel to learn about the musical cultures of the world. It is essential that we understand people in a more complete, cultural way through music, the arts, cuisine, and religious and philosophical beliefs and practices. In my view, experiencing people's musical expressions may be one of the most direct avenues to intercultural understanding.

Given the great variety of musical expressions available for representation within the curriculum, how does a teacher choose an expression while also maintaining its musical integrity?

It's not wise for a teacher to do a quick job of coming into too many cultures all at once. Patience and gradual immersion into a musical culture other than one's own is probably the best course to take. There is much to be learned from the juxtaposition of the teacher's first musical culture with a second one he or she selects for study. What then may result is an understanding by comparison of the two musical cultures. This comparison becomes an enriching multicultural (or at least bicultural) experience for the teacher and, ultimately, the students.

What could be the harm of teaching a musical culture we do not know well?

We may misinterpret a musical culture we have not spent time with (through listening, performing, and studying its cultural meaning). Certainly, some teaching can proceed with less study. Teachers can present, for example, the sounds and names of instruments from India without having studied them much. The danger comes when we start trying to transpose notes onto a blackboard for students when the tradition is, in fact, an oral one and when Western staff notation cannot appropriately convey the intricacies of pitch and rhythm. We can get carried away with trying to transform the music of a given culture into Western conceptions of it.

When we know something of a variety of musical cultures, how should we approach their presentation to students?

It's always important for teachers to teach their strengths and to feature musical pieces and cultures in which they have solid knowledge and training. Then, they can present musical experiences derived from people living in Asia, Africa, South America, and Mexico, for example. Listening and performing experiences in a variety of musical cultures may reduce "musical bias," the kind of attitude that develops among children who think that Bach is more important than Mexican *jarocho* music. [See the Musical Styles sidebar for a definition of *jarocho* and other terms related to Latino music.]

Should teachers strive for "authenticity" in the musical experiences they provide their students?

There is no such thing as a static or totally stabilized "authentic" music. A performance may be authentic for "what it is," whether the music be traditional or currently popular. But, once you take the music out of its cultural context, it's no longer authentic:

A mariachi band usually includes guitarists, violinists, and trumpeters.

it adapts to its new surroundings. Take Afro-Cuban music, for example. If you perform a rumba instrumentally but with no vocal part and no dancing, are you really doing a rumba? The rhythms of the claves and the conga are very traditional, but without the essential interplay of singing, dancing, and pantomiming with the instrumental parts, the rumba is incomplete. The music is authentic for "what it is" (since the rumba, like much music, is not frozen), but it is not the traditional rumba style or form. It is important to inform students of this distinction by noting, "Look, what we're doing here is *close* to the tradition, but not exact. Listen to the real thing."

What is the musical culture of your own expertise?

I study the music of Mexico (and Mexican Americans), the Caribbean, especially Cuba, and Latin America at large (including Latinos in the U.S.). [See the map in figure 1.] I'm currently working with artist Tito Puente, studying Latin music in New York through his eyes.

Are there similarities among these Latin musical cultures?

In the U.S., many Latinos with roots in the Caribbean, Mexico, and elsewhere gravitate toward popular Latin styles, particularly *tropical,* Caribbean, and salsa styles. My inter-

Figure 1. Mexico, Central America, and the Caribbean

Selected Recordings

Mexican

Los Bukis: Mi volvi a acordar de ti. FonoVisa FPCD-5103. Melody. Soft *cumbia* dance music (the most popular Mexican record ever).

Los Lobos: La pistola y el corazón. Slash/Warner Bros. 4-25790-2. 1988 recording by leading Chicano band of Latino-based rock music.

Los Mariachis: An Introduction to Mexican Mariachi Music. World Music Press. Book with tape that features analysis and synthesis of a single mariachi piece.

Mariachi Aguilas de Chapala. Folkways FW 8870. Includes well-known *sones* like "Jarabe tapatio," "La bamba," "La Adelita," "Ay, Jalisco, no te raajes," and "Las mañanitas."

Mexico—Fiestas. Elektra Nonesuch H-72070. Village festivals in southern Mexico, including marimba ensembles and brass bands.

The Real Mexico. Elektra Nonesuch H-72009. Fiesta music and songs of Tarascan Indians and mestizos of Michoacán state.

Canciones de mi padre. Asylum 60765-2. Linda Ronstadt sings *ranchera* classics to the accompaniment of Mariachi Vargas.

Caribbean

Irakere: Misa negra. Rounder R1886R. Salsa with a contemporary jazz treatment, played by Cuba's most successful contemporary group.

La Sonora Poncena: Soul of Puerto Rico. Charly LR990. Well-known salsa pieces played by trumpet-led brass sections.

Sabroso. Virgin/Earthworks 91312. Compilation of salsa and other dances played by known bands in Cuba.

Other Latino

Caliente = Hot. New World NW 244. Latino music in New York.

El Conguero: Pancho Sanchez. Concord-Picante CJP-286. Latin jazz, with emphasis on conga drums.

La Familia: Pancho Sanchez. Picante CCD-4369. Latin jazz—includes "Mambo Inn" and "Senegal."

Fania All Stars: Live at Yankee Stadium, vols. 1 and 2. Fania. Columbia CR75L. Classic salsa pieces in New York, featuring soloists Celia Cruz, Ruben Blades, Ray Barretto, and Eddie Palmieri.

Steve Loza Sextet: Red Car Blues. Merrimack MR 10102. Latin jazz, by a group from Los Angeles's east side.

Understanding Latin Rhythms, vols. 1, 2. L. P. Ventures LPV-337. Recordings of Latin rhythms on percussion instruments, with notation.

Un Poco Loco: Tito Puente. Picante CCD-4329. Features music for Latin jazz ensemble and orchestra, including "El timbalon."

ests include these popular Latin styles and also what we call "Latin jazz," which evolved in the Puerto Rican, Cuban, and Dominican communities of New York and which is increasingly popular among Mexican, Central American, and other Latin populations in the U.S. The Latin American musical identity is very much wrapped up in this Afro-Cuban (and other) tropical dance music.

What is the incidence of Mexicans, Caribbean peoples, and other Latinos in the U.S.?

There is a great diversity of Latinos in the U.S., but the proportions of countries and cultures represented in one city or the other vary considerably. Chicanos live in Los Angeles and other areas of California, in the Southwest, and in other parts of the West. (The many Mexican Americans in Texas often refer to themselves as "Tejanos.") On the east coast, Puerto Ricans and Cubans have lived for generations in New York, Philadelphia, Hartford, and elsewhere and were joined a bit later by Dominicans. Large communities of Cubans, Haitians, and other Caribbean peoples are found in Miami, Tampa, other areas of Florida, and other parts of the Southeast. Central Americans reside mostly in Los Angeles, with other Latin American groups diffused throughout the U.S.

What is the meaning and function of music among Latin Americans?

Music is an essential part of Latin American culture. A Chicano "city" or neighborhood is a place of weddings, *bautismos* (baptisms), *bailes* (dances), *velorios* (wakes, or night parties), and patriotic "enchilada dinners." At all of these occasions, *familias* (families) and *compadres* (friends) share in making music, singing, and dancing to the lively sounds of an assortment of instrumental groups. It's interesting that when you ask Latinos to name their heroes and heroines, they often mention the musicians whose music they enjoy.

What is the place of dance in Latino communities?

As compared to "mainstream" American culture, dance is more essen-

Lesson Plan for a Chicano Poem

Objectives

Students will:

■ listen to the recited poem with its rhythmic ostinati accompaniment

■ discuss the meaning of the poem

■ learn to play the rhythmic ostinati on percussion instruments

■ learn to recite the poem rhythmically, with percussion accompaniment

Materials

■ "The Hands," from *Steve Loza Sextet: Red Car Blues,* Merrimack MR 10102

■ Cowbell, mallet

■ Sticks or claves

■ Conga drums

Procedures

1. Listen to the recording of the poem "The Hands." Although students will undoubtedly be attracted to the rhythmic accompaniment of the percussion instruments, ask them to listen also to the words of the poem (shown on the opposite page). Ask them to listen and be able to identify Spanish language words and names of Latin instruments. (In the third stanza, *albondigas* are Mexican-style meatballs in a soup.)

2. Explain that "The Hands" was written by Gina Valdes, one of the most important contemporary Chicano poets. Show the entire text of the poem on an overhead transparency. Discuss the intent of the poem to express the soul of the struggle for Chicano (and, in general, Latin) people in the U.S. to receive recognition and equal rights. Invite students to select phrases that describe particularly Latin images ("clap to the beat of corn on its way to becoming a tortilla") or images of manual labor (hands tied "to brooms, mops, trays, and dusters" and "they … plant corn, mint, hope, and cilantro").

3. Listen to the selection again. Direct students to maintain a steady beat on their desktops or laps. Add sticks or claves and the cowbell. The cowbell is played at the small end (outside), with the other hand spread across the bottom to mute the sound. Add the conga drum part, played by flat hands spread across the head of the drum. (See below for the notated rhythm.) Note that, except for the introduction, the rhythm tends not to change much; it is mostly an ostinato pattern combined with the keeping of the pulse.

4. Listen to the recording again. While following the text, note where the speaker gives accent to certain words, speeds or slows the tempo of his recitation, and takes a breath. Practice reciting the poem rhythmically as a large group, individually, or in small groups (one for each stanza). A choral recitation can be rehearsed, with occasional solos as determined by the class group. Add percussion instruments as accompaniment.

Introduction

Cowbell, Sticks, and Conga:

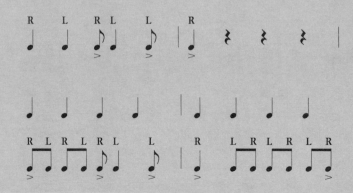

Throughout

Cowbell, Sticks:

Conga:

"The Hands" by Gina Valdes

(*Introduction—4 measures of instrumental music*)

Depending on the light of the hairy sun or the moon
Or the shade of the tamarinded noon or the chapel at dusk,
The hands, these hands, my hands, your hands,
Will appear cream or cinnamon, pink, red, black, or yellow.
Our heritage.

These are hands of congas, of requintos, guiros, claves, bongos and tim-
    bales,
Of maracas, charangos, guitarrones, and marimbas, castanets, tam-
    bourines, and cymbals.
Tin-tin-timbalao, tingo.
These hands sing, dance, clap to the beat of corn
On its way to becoming a tortilla.

These hands around albondigas and dreams
Circle waists, sides, and hips,
Peel bananas, masks, and mangos,
Add, subtract, multiply on blackboards, beds and griddles.

These hands speak fluent Spanish.
They warm. They reduce fevers.
Sometimes they write poetry.
Sometimes they recite it.
These hands could take away all pain.

These hands tied by centuries of rope to ovens, tables, and to diapers,
To brooms, mops, trays, and dusters,
To saws and hammers, to picks, hoes, and shovels.
They scrub floors, plates, and lies,
Pick strawberries, grapes, insults, and onions.
Plant corn, mint, hope, and cilantro.
Piece by piece, they honor us with our history.

These hands, so large, so small,
Two hummingbirds, quiet, still, joined, pierced by a nail of U.S. steel.
Unbind, shout, close into a fist of sorrow, of anger, of impatience.
These raised hands open, demand the same as they produce, as they are
    giving.
These hands smile in triumph.

(*Closing—8 measures of instrumental music*)

Source: Gina Valdes, "The Hands," from *Comiendo Lumbre: Eating Fire.* © 1985 by Maize Press. Used by permission.

tial to Latino communities. During the swing era fifty years ago, dance was the epitome of musical participation among the general mainstream American population. Now, however, Americans watch music as it is made, while in the Latino community, dance is still strong—an essential part of social life and family life as well.

■ ■ ■ ■ ■

Latin American cultures are singing cultures.

■ ■ ■ ■ ■

Is there a single musical style that represents Latin Americans?

There is tremendous diversity among Latin American musical styles, with European, African, and indigenous elements forming separate musical cultures and also influencing musical fusions. Latino cultures are not homogeneous. There are culturally attached styles that are quite localized within each country and region of Latin America, and many of them are carried to the U.S. Yet, there is also internationally popular, commercialized Latin American music. Salsa music and pop/rock music with a Latino flavor are known throughout most Latino communities in the U.S. [See the "Latin America and the Caribbean" chapter in *Multicultural Perspectives in Music Education* (MENC, 1989).]

Is there a single musical style that represents Mexican or Chicano culture?

In Mexico alone, there is a wide diversity of regional cultures. There are many regions: Chiapas, Chihuahua, Jalisco, Oaxaca, Veracruz, for example. Music in Mexico includes the popular *banda* music, but also mariachi music, *tropical* music, *norteño* music, *ranchera* music (espe-

Lesson Plan for a Mariachi "Son"

Objectives

Students will:

- sing a mariachi *son* (an instrumental piece with singing, associated with dance)

- play a guitar strum that features a hemiola rhythm

- move to the hemiola rhythm while singing

- identify hemiola rhythms in mariachi music

Materials

- Selections from the recording *Mariachi Aguilas de Chapala* (*The Mariachi Band: Eagles of Chapala*), Folkways FW 8870

- "El tirador" ("The Marksman") from *Los Mariachis: An Introduction to Mexican Mariachi Music* (tape/book) by Patricia Harpole, Mark Fogelquist, and El Mariachi Uclatlan (Danbury, CT: World Music Press, 1989)

- guitars

- maracas, claves

Procedures

1. Listen to examples of mariachi music from the recording *Mariachi Aguilas de Chapala*. Particularly well-known *sones* are "Jarabe tapatio," "La bamba," "La Adelita," "Ay, Jalisco, no te raajes," and "Las mañanitas." As students listen informally over a period of several class sessions, direct their attention to similarities among the selections (e.g., the instrumentation and the 6/8 or 12/8 hemiola rhythm organized in subdivisions of 3-3-2-2-2).

2. Describe the mariachi ensemble as an instrumental ensemble centered in the state of Jalisco, in and around Guadalajara (the second largest city in Mexico). Its origins are in mestizo (mixed) music of Spanish, Indian, and African influence that was performed in villages and towns in the nineteenth century. Early mariachi ensembles included harp, violins, guitar or vihuela (small guitar), and voices. The *guitarrón* replaced the harp about 1900 in providing a stronger bass part, and trumpets were added by the 1930s. Mariachi bands may vary in size from about seven to fourteen members.

3. While listening to "El tirador," pat or tap the rhythm of the guitar and vihuela strums. "Play" the pulses, including accents, on laps, desktops, or floor, alternating the right and left hands—see the rhythmic notation below. Later, "play" just the accented pulses 3-3-2-2-2:

4. Sing the melody of "El tirador" on "la," following the music on the opposite page. Then, pronounce the words in rhythm:

> Soy tee-rah-dor kayah lahs ah-vays lays tee-roh voh-lahn-doh.

> Chah-pah-ree-tah day mee vee-dah pohr tooah-mohr ahn-doh pay-nahn-doh.

5. Give the translation of the text. Note the Spanish words for marksman ("tirador"), birds ("aves"), and little one ("chaparrita"):

> I am a marksman who shoots at flying birds.

> Little one of my life, for you I am suffering.

6. Listen again to "El tirador." In the air, "strum" the rhythm of the guitar and vihuela, alternating down (D) and up (U) strokes. Accent the first pulse of each 2- or 3-stroke unit:

7. Practice playing this strum on guitar, using the G and D⁷ chords. If the rhythm is uncertain, reinforce the hemiola rhythm by returning to no. 3 and no. 6 above.

8. Divide the group into singers and players, and perform the first verse of "El tirador." Switch parts.

9. Standing, step to the accented first duration of the hemiola rhythm. Start with the weight on the left foot, chanting while stepping. It may be necessary to chant first, and to chant while patting or clapping, before proceeding to the chant/step combination:

10. Divide group into guitarists, singers, and dancers. Dancers form partners in a circle. Partners stand side by side facing left (clockwise) and step the pattern practiced in no. 9 above. Girls (on the inside) can rustle

their full skirts, while boys (outside) may lay their right arms horizontally across their waists and left arms across their backs. Singers and guitarists stand to one side in performance. Maracas or claves can be added to reinforce the hemiola rhythm and to unify the ensemble.

11. Listen to other mariachi selections from the *Mariachi Aguilas de Chapala* recording. Identify the occurrence of hemiola rhythms by patting, tapping, or clapping them as they occur.

"El tirador"

Source: "El tirador" from *Los Mariachis: An Introduction to Mexican Mariachi Music* by Patricia Harpole, Mark Fogelquist, and El Mariachi Uclatlan. © 1989 by World Music Press. Used by permission. (Song has been transposed by P. S. Campbell.)

---

cially among the working class), salsa music, *jarocho* music, and *huapango* music. [See the Latino Musical Styles sidebar for brief descriptions.] All of these are Mexican musics, and all of these musics can be found in the U.S.

How do Latin American children learn the music of their heritage?

In Latin America, children have a propensity for singing in their earliest childhood. This may be due to the fact that music is pervasive in the home, with recordings playing and people singing. Latin American cultures are singing cultures. I remember my older brother, at the age of five, learning Mexican *rancheras* as he listened to recordings of Jose Alfredo Jimenez (translating the Spanish words into English as he went). Music saturates the home, and children are thus musically enculturated. [See the Selected Recordings sidebar.]

If music is pervasive, does it play a part in the bilingual education of Chicano children in the U.S.?

Beyond the music at home, in church, and at parties, music is often incorporated by bilingual educators in the Los Angeles schools to teach language and cultural concepts. Singing games are frequently taught in two languages, so that the meaning of one language is gained without the loss of the other (the first) language.

Have you any final thoughts for teachers who are contemplating the teaching of Latin American music?

I think we're on the verge of a very exciting era in American education when music can be powerful enough to captivate the attention of students, who then learn music as well as culture. Music is a tremendous thing in any culture, and its transcending of the more familiar verbal mode of communication is one of its major strengths. We live in a "close" world so our attempts to help young people understand the cultural matrix of which they are a part must include music and the arts. Intercultural understanding through music is worth striving for. ■

POSTLUDE

The eight interviews are telling of musical and pedagogical issues, both for world music at large and within the context of particular ethnic cultures. Two North American musical cultures were featured (McAllester's Navajo and Burnim's African American gospel), and Loza's comments on Latino music emanated from his research on Hispanic cultures of Mexico, the Caribbean, and southern California. Other world regions were represented as well: Miller's Thailand, with reference to other Southeast Asian cultures; Nettl's Iran and, more generally, the Middle East; Yung's China and Chinese music in Hong Kong; Waterman's focus on the Yoruba of Nigeria, with reference to other western and central African cultures; and Seeger's Suya people of the Amazon region in Brazil, one of the world's smaller populations living in a region of subsistence resources. These cultures represent just the "tip of the iceberg" when considering the multitude of musical cultures in the world. While one or more cultures from the Americas, Africa, and Asia were addressed, however briefly, other cultures and large geographic regions (and even continents) were bypassed.

The intent of the series, however, was not to provide a comprehensive compendium of all the world's musical cultures for teachers and students. Nor

is this collection a methods or materials book for teachers; a more appropriate source for such information is *Multicultural Perspectives in Music Education* (1989, 1996). Rather, the aim of the project was to allow a forum for the presentation and discussion of issues relevant to world music and multicultural music education. The perspectives of scholars with much to offer about particular styles and traditions of music were tapped, the results of which could also afford a look at "the big picture" of world music in K–12 and collegiate instructional settings. Indeed, it is intriguing to come to terms with music's functions and values in various contexts and to understand it as a human phenomenon. But for teachers, the contribution of *Music in Cultural Context* is more likely an understanding of ways in which such issues as teaching competence, musical authenticity, cultural representation, musical traditions and changes, and contextualization are articulated by specialists, so that these thoughts can be weighed and considered in the future design of appropriate musical education for young people.

When perspectives are shared by experts in any field, a reader's natural reaction is to inquire as to the similarities that unite them and the distinctions that define them. Thematic issues probed through the course of

the eight interviews are examined below, and the ethnomusicologists' individual opinions and occasions of group consensus are noted. It is here that this collection becomes "more than a sum of parts" of the *MEJ* series, for the discussion that follows reveals the conceptual patterns encountered at the crossroads of music education, ethnomusicology, and world music.

The Place of World Music in the Curriculum

Of the general questions posed as openers to each interview, the matter of whether the world's musical cultures should be taught to elementary and secondary school students was raised. This broad question was followed by more focused ones: If so, when? Where? As might be expected, all eight ethnomusicologists were in favor of the inclusion of a more varied musical palette in the school curriculum. Perhaps in recognition of the limited musical diet of undergraduate studies and teacher education programs, McAllester advised that, for school children taught by traditionally trained teachers, "It's better to learn anything about other cultures ... than nothing at all." Likewise, Nettl encouraged teachers to begin to teach world musics as well as they could: "Some things are worth doing—even when they are not done too well—until, through further study, they can be done better." As for when, several noted that the time for students' exposure to and training in the world's musical cultures could begin at an early age, even "as early as possible" (according to Yung and Waterman), presumably in preschool and throughout the primary grades.

Those interviewed did not hesitate in naming the music portion of the school curriculum as the appropriate place for the study of world musics. Still, Nettl noted that music of the world's cultures should also "make an appearance in the social science curriculum—geography, history, and social studies classes." Similarly, Seeger thought that "it should not be kept isolated in the music curriculum." He suggested that music be included within the larger world studies curriculum; in this way, the study of India or Brazil and its Amazonian rain forest could be amplified or enhanced through musical experiences, just as slavery could be studied through field hollars and the immigration of Vietnamese or Cambodians could be understood through a comparison of music "in the homeland and as it has changed over time in the U.S." Such curricular study may require a team of teachers, or minimally, the interface of a social studies or classroom teacher with a music specialist.

Of particular interest to teachers engaged in curricular redesign is the juxtaposition of world music with Western art music. Loza claimed that teachers "owe it to [them]selves to be multicultural in the musical education of young people," and should consider that "musical bias" could be reduced through listening and performing experiences that span a variety of cultures. He suggested continuous exposure to many musical styles. Waterman noted that one essential aim of education, the development of critical thought, could be accomplished as students are led to listen to assorted musical styles in discerning ways and to express reasons for their acceptance (or rejection) of musical sounds and styles. Miller described education's aim as one of opening "new doors for students," and then directed teachers to avoid starting

with Western art music as a "base camp" for students' musical education. As he explained it, "Western art music then becomes the universal standard by which all other music is measured"—not an approach Miller would advocate.

Likewise, Nettl warned against the provision of lessons in Western art music before moving on to other kinds of music as a secondary activity. Instead, he recommended "parity of the world's musical cultures" at all stages, by featuring some kind of intercultural group of concepts and sounds. The treatment of melody across several traditions or the function of music at work and in worship illustrate the comparative approach to which Nettl referred. Yung maintained that "non-Western music" is much less accessible to young people and thus "must be given a special 'sell'" by teachers who seek to ensure "equal playing time" of world music with Western music. McAllester's view was that Western European art music may not be a necessity for some students, or "something that we feel we should have to teach in our school system to everybody regardless." His explanation was direct: "It is only one music of many."

Musical Knowledge and Competence

Once persuaded of the value of infusing more of the world's musics within the curricular studies of elementary and secondary schools, teachers are confronted with the challenges of developing their own knowledge and skills in styles beyond their earlier training and experience. Typical responses to the question of which channels teachers might pursue for information on musical cultures of the world were "listening" and "reading." Collegiate textbooks that survey many musical cultures were high on the list of recommended readings, in particular *Worlds of Music* (Jeff Todd Titon, ed., Schirmer Books, 1994) and *Excursions in World Music* (Bruno Nettl et al., Prentice-Hall, 1992). Several mentioned the journal *Ethnomusicology*, and culture-specific texts were suggested through the course of the interview (or were compiled by me).

See the bibliography for a wide assortment of texts, and the interview articles for culture-specific resources. Listening was discussed as key to the development of teachers' (and students') competence. Waterman raised the issue of "informed listening," hearing combined with thinking about how the music is put together. Many referred to contexts and sources for listening, including radio stations, live concerts, community festivals, and recordings in university and public libraries.

Knowledge and competence, however, may require investigation of other channels of information as well. Miller suggested not only listening and reading, but also studying videotapes and visiting various "communities to experience musical culture." He recommended that teachers learn music and culture by attending summer festivals, religious celebrations, and New Year's parties. Seeger advised not only local festivals, but also "going out to meet people and, if they live locally, asking them to participate in the classroom experience." Even closer to home, he noted that students' own parents may be repositories of musical culture and could be tapped by teachers.

The acquisition of knowledge of unfamiliar musical cultures cannot shortcut a considerable time commitment on the part of the teacher. Nettl commented that "there's no way of teaching music (of the world's cultures) without 'putting in time,'" and Miller admitted that a "crash course" has serious limitations on the knowledge that can be gained in a short time. Better than workshops and short courses is a "carefully structured master's degree" (Nettl), or some other more extended period of study. As Burnim suggested, perhaps every musical tradition merits the "years of study" it takes teachers to become skilled in Western European art music. Loza's perspective is noteworthy: "Patience and gradual immersion into a musical culture other than one's own is probably the best course to take." At any rate, while musical knowledge and skills are attainable, they require the dedicated teacher's time and effort.

Musical Authenticity

One of the chief concerns of music educators has been the issue of authenticity, both in regard to the selection of music that can be considered representative of a culture and its actual performance by people from outside the culture. Interestingly, authenticity was deemed by some of the ethnomusicologists interviewed as having minimal importance. Yung explained: "I almost never use 'authentic' to discuss the music of China because it implies absolute values" that are nonexistent within so historically long and culturally varied a nation. He explained that authenticity is difficult to prove in an objective manner and that most Chinese musical genres and instruments can be traced back far enough to earlier, often foreign, influences. He posed the weighty question: "Where is one to draw the cut-off line" between the authentic and pure music and the music that has been borrowed, adapted, and accepted as their own by the people of a designated culture?

Seeger defined music that is "historically identified with a community" as traditional and "music that has been introduced" to a culture as nontraditional, yet authentic. He cited the introduction of music through the work of missionaries or military enforcement as examples of nontraditional music, but nonetheless music that may have become fully integrated within a culture. Authentic music is that which people possess as their own—music that is "genuine" to them as listeners and performers. Salsa music can be (and is) performed as authentically by the Thai as it is by Puerto Ricans in San Juan and Cubans in Miami, just as Beethoven is embraced as fully by performers in Baghdad, Buenos Aires, and Boston as by those who live in Bonn or Vienna. Thus, the Suya of the Amazonian rain forest were able to learn "Pretty Polly" from Seeger in the early 1970s, to enjoy it enough to add it to their own musical repertoire, and to sing it so easily again with him two decades later. Music can be introduced to a culture, and then can be performed "authentically," or changed by way of "accents" and interpretations that an

ethnic-cultural group may give it.

Loza pushed the authenticity concept a step further, proclaiming that "there is no such thing as a static or totally stabilized 'authentic' music." He explained that a performance is authentic "for what it is, whether the music be traditional or currently popular." Further, as McAllester observed, "Any culture is constantly in flux, with new ideas coming into vogue." Music is seldom frozen in time, unchanging, and untouched by the influences from beyond the cultural core.

For teachers, authenticity is a challenge confronted daily in the design and delivery of instruction to students. Perhaps Loza's practical words on authenticity are among the most useful; he advised teachers to inform their students of the distinctions between traditional and changing, nontraditional styles. Teachers might direct students' attention to the similarities and differences between their performance and that of those from the culture by saying (as did Loza), "Look, what we're doing here is *close* to the tradition, but not exact. Listen to the real thing." By extension, students can be led to perform a singing game from Japan or a rhythmic percussion piece from Ghana, and taught to listen in a critical-comparative manner to the similarities and differences between their own performance and that of people from the tradition.

An authentic performance of a given musical piece or style by students is always a goal worth achieving. Authenticity is closely linked to careful listening, so that a musically acceptable rendition of the song, form, or style can be rendered by students in a classroom or ensemble. McAllester suggested that Native American music be sung "in a somewhat more nasal voice than we do. If you had a recording, you would hear that and could imitate it." Burnim accepted that "listening to recordings is a valuable and important experience" for learning gospel music, and pressed even further, noting that the complexities of the style—and of the performer-audience interplay—necessitate the learning of gospel music within the full context of a live performance within a church service. Water-

man commented that for students who hoped to perform in the style of "Kansas City jazz, Korean singing, or west African drumming," a combination of careful listening and mimesis (imitation) might be the most likely way to close in on an acceptable, if not completely authentic, performance.

Representative Music

Which music represents a group of people? Given the tremendous time constraints of the music program (for example, the 60- or even 30-minute weekly class in an elementary school), the choice of a single song or musical work for performance, listening, and study becomes one of the most important decisions a teacher can make. When sampled, this choice may be the single musical image held by students as the musical expression of a group of people. But which age group is represented by the musical selection? Region? Socioeconomic class? Religious affiliation? Imagine singling out one American musical work to represent the nation: a shape-note song, a choral hymn by William Billings, Duke Ellington's "Take the 'A' Train," Charles Ives's *New England Triptych,* a Sioux Indian social dance song, "Yankee Doodle," a croon-tune by Elvis Presley, Leonard Bernstein's "(I'd Like to Be in) America," a segment of Aaron Copland's *Appalachian Spring,* an African American spiritual, or Bruce Springsteen's "Born in the U.S.A." Each choice reflects a particular time in U.S. history, as well as a cultural group based upon age, social class, ethnicity, and other factors.

Just as the "representation" issue is a difficult one for teachers, so it is for scholars.[1] For the Navajo, any one of hundreds of squaw dance songs or Enemyway dance songs was McAllester's suggestion of a "single, most representative" musical genre. Seeger described two principal genres of music among the Suya: "a low unison song sung by adult men" and "shout songs" sung by individual boys and men. Yung acknowledged the difficulty of choosing genres, but then named Chinese opera, narrative song, and instrumental music as best representing China. Among the Yoruba of Nigeria, Waterman called the music played by the dundun talking drum as "emblematic of their culture," and later explained the importance of pop styles like juju (with its fusion of traditional Yoruba and foreign features with contemporary technologies) as also quite representative of the culture.

Burnim's response to the "most representative" question was richly layered. She clarified that "traditional gospel music is still the major force" and named Mahalia Jackson and the Roberta Martin Singers as examples of gospel pioneers. She then listed numerous artists of contemporary gospel, including "youth market" groups like A-1 Swift. Burnim explained that representative gospel style "is not easy to name" because of its continuous evolution. Later, she listed concepts, characteristics, and a further list of gospel composers and performers that constitute minimal knowledge of the style that every student should possess.

Loza selected "salsa music and pop/rock music with a Latino flavor" as the music that is best known in Latino communities in the U.S., but not before explaining something of the diversity among Latin American musical styles. He asserted that "Latino cultures are not homogeneous," and that each country and region of Latin American has its own local style.

Miller and Nettl raised the issue of preferred music versus music that serves in an official capacity as the "national identity" music. Miller noted that while young Thai people listen to American-derived rock music and others listen to regional folk and popular music, the classical style of the piphat court ensemble (of xylophones, gongs, shawm, and drums) is singled out as the official national music of Thailand by government officials and Thai who live abroad. Iranians hold a similar sentiment, such that while they may listen to folk and popular music, they say about classical Persian music, "Ah, that's the music of our nation," according to Nettl.

The representative genres named may be featured in listening lessons, and some may be performed in part or in full (for example, salsa by a jazz ensemble, gospel by a choir, and dundun patterns by a percussion group). On the other hand, the use of certain genres or pieces was cautioned, some less for lack of representation than for their musical complexity or because of their integration with particular belief systems and religious rituals that might prove inappropriate within school settings. Ceremonial songs and other religious music (of any culture) were viewed as poor or precarious fits within the curriculum (according to McAllester and Seeger). Miller advised against national anthems, since "they're almost never typical of the country" and may even "present a political problem to immigrants who may not recognize the present government" of the nation they left behind. "High-art music," according to Seeger, might also be best left out of a performance-oriented curriculum. The music of Chinese pipa or Indian vina, for example, like the study of violin and piano, requires considerable training in conservatory-like settings and should not be included within the realm of school programs whose time restrictions do not allow for the technical training required of this music.

Cultural Context

The contextualization of music is often subject to heated debate among teachers. How much descriptive information should be provided of the people from whom the music derives in order to understand the meaning, function, and value of their music? When does music instruction, supplemented by maps, chronologies of cultural events, discussions of current political and economic affairs, presentations of the visual arts, and discussions of literature and folklore, turn into a social studies lesson? Responses to these questions varied.

Waterman's discussion of Yoruba music was permeated with mention of its cultural meaning. He admitted that their "music is closely bound up with kinship, religion, politics, and economics," and in describing the contents of a lesson, recommended that teachers point out the function of a musical piece and allow students time to reflect upon the meaning of a song's lyrics. His description of Yoruba contemporary music was grounded in its societal context. Equally convincing of the importance of embedding music within its cultural frame was Miller's question: "What's the purpose of playing Thai melodies on specially tuned xylophones if students don't know where Thailand is or *what* it is?" He recommended setting the music in its geographic and historical context and providing students with some knowledge of the music makers themselves. Burnim's listing of "what students in American schools should know about gospel music" included not only composers and concepts, but also contextual matters: "They should understand something of the history of African American religious music and its role and importance in the lives of African Americans."

Yung's perspective keenly illustrated something of the polarity of views held by ethnomusicologists on certain issues. He adamantly opposed contextualization, recalling his own youth in China and Hong Kong when he was learning Western art music: "No one gave me information of the cultural background or context of the music, but by listening I developed a sense of what was 'good music.'" He maintained that verbal knowledge about music is less important than the sound itself, and claimed that "an emphasis on the cultural and social background" may even block students' opportunities to develop a closeness with the music.

McAllester recalled the Navajo ceremonial practitioner who, when asked whether squaw dance music and peyote music could be used in the classroom, responded with another question: "Why do it? It would be out of context." This led to McAllester's pondering of the issue of education at large as out of context, "*as if* you were an engineer or *as if* you were a mathematician." Neither he nor the ceremonial practitioner objected to the decontextualization of the music, but both raised the issue of its usefulness when removed from its typical setting. Loza's statement bridges the issues of authenticity and context, and is apropos here: "Once you take the music out of its cultural context, it's no longer authentic."

Thus, there are several views posed here on the extent to which cultural context could be provided by teachers to clarify music's meaning. Perhaps, the solution is neither "all context" nor "none at all," but rather, some midpoint in between. No doubt, music should be the main feature of a music lesson, whether performed, listened to, studied, and/or responded to in some way. However, a few minutes spent on "setting the scene" of the culture from which the music derives may be useful, so that students understand it more fully. Who performs it? When? Where? What do the instruments look like? Of what materials are they made? How does geography and climate affect the construction of the instruments? How was this music taught and learned? What do you "do" with the music, as an audience member—listen, dance, clap along, sing? Is it music preferred by young people? By some adult group? This information can be provided efficiently through photographs, video clips, or brief comments in and around the actual musical experience. The music itself can initiate such questions and should reign supreme throughout the course of the class.[2]

Cultural Views of Music for Children

Certainly some of the recurring questions in an examination of musical cultures by educators pertain to music that children learn—or are taught—by other children, through the media, and in the schools. Not surprisingly, children's music was not often a key concern among ethnomusicologists interviewed during the course of their own fieldwork; adult music, both amateur and professional, was more often the focus of their research. Still, a number of observations were offered as to the repertoire and musical education of children and young people within the eight musical cultures surveyed.

Beyond the schools, at home, on playgrounds, and through worship services, children typically acquire the music of their parents' (and adult) culture. McAllester remarked that while there is no music among the Navajo designed specifically for children, they "just pick up songs that they've heard

from the adults and sing parts of them." Nettl made similar observations, noting that "in traditional Iran, children listen to and participate in adult music right from the beginning." He explained that since parents bring their children to social events where adult music is performed, they readily learn this music such that "there is not as much of a need" for children to develop their own separate children's music. The Suya also learn the music of adults and may even "have their own ceremonies after the adults are finished" with theirs, during which they incorporate the music they have heard (according to Seeger).

Yung observed that children in China who are motivated to become more musical do so by watching adults perform and then imitating them. Many more, Yung claimed, learn music from television, video, karaoke sets, cassette tapes, and CDs. Waterman observed that the singing games and songs of Yoruba children are "not markedly different from the mainstream of Yoruba music," (i.e., the music made by adults). He recalled his observations of Yoruba children who "imitate pop music styles, using cardboard boxes, tin cans, pen caps, and other discarded objects." Among African American children, many "sing gospel music from the time they're old enough to feel secure singing," first in children's choirs and then in youth groups (according to Burnim). Loza broadly referred to Latin American cultures as "singing cultures" and reasoned that Latino children "have a propensity for singing…due to the fact that music is pervasive in the home."

Few schools in these cultures place music within their curricular studies. In Thailand, music is not a required subject. Children learn traditional and popular songs from their teachers in school, but the national curriculum in the arts is rarely put into practice. There are exceptions, however, as in the case of the secondary school Miller described where children learn to play Thai classical music before their regular classes in the early morning. As for Iran, despite some earlier attempts to establish appreciation classes in Western music, music instruction in Iran-

ian schools is nearly nil (according to Nettl). Navajo children learn standard American songs from textbooks, but also "increasingly now, squaw dance songs" (according to McAllester). In China, Yung recalled that children learn folks songs at school and "specially composed children's songs, many of which are based upon Western major and minor tonalities." As for the Yoruba of Nigeria, children learn songs at primary school and in church, often Yoruba lyrics set to European melodies (according to Waterman). In any case, there were few instances reported of a thorough or continuous musical education within these cultures or of a culture's art, classical, or other "serious" music being transmitted to children within the schools. Such musical training may occur "on the outside" in special schools and institutes or through apprenticeship systems.

Teaching the World's Musical Cultures

While ethnomusicologists are expert in their knowledge of one or more musical cultures, many have teaching expertise as well. Theories and practices of instruction and curriculum (particularly at the K–12 level) are not usually their specialized training, and yet many can speak from experience on ways of teaching the world's musical cultures. The following are suggestions for just that, taken from these interviews and conversations with other ethnomusicologists, with some extensions. These suggestions are meant to help teachers who contemplate changes and revisions to the content and delivery of their classes.

1. *Blend the "old" with the "new."* Do not discard the repertoires for children, choirs, bands, and orchestras that have been successful for you and your students. Rather, add to them, including selections from the array of cultures for which recordings, sourcebooks, and scores are available.

2. *Listen.* Before selecting music—and most certainly before teaching—listen carefully to recordings. Listen for the stylistic nuances of the music (and the text, when available) and to the pitch inflections, rhythmic features, stops and starts, and expressive components. Be prepared to listen

more than a few times, and as many as sixty or seventy times, so that the music penetrates your musical mind and ear.

3. *Practice.* Whether on the brink of teaching a children's singing game, rhythms for a percussion ensemble, a circle dance, a gospel song in four-part harmony, or a montuno for a salsa number, try it out. Sing it, chant it, and play it until it "feels right." No music can be performed or taught (which typically requires the teacher's demonstration at the very least) without concentrated time spent in the repeated yet thoughtful practice of it.

4. *Teach comparatively, in a "world music" manner.* Just as Nettl organized musical selections around specific concepts and elements, focus, for example, on seven-beat meter or Dorian mode and find musical illustrations from a variety of world cultures for students' performance, listening, and study.

5. *Teach fewer cultures in greater depth.* As Miller suggested, a significant impact can be made on students' development if more concentrated time in the curriculum were given to fewer musical traditions. Broad surveys have their place on the educational continuum, but knowing the musical traditions of two (or three or four) cultures well enough to be able to perform them appropriately and listen to them with knowledge of structures and meanings is a noble goal in any educational setting.

6. *Supply limited contextual information.* Music does not exist in a vacuum;

the performance or study of a song, work, or style can be made more meaningful when a brief reference to its context is provided. Music should always the centerpiece, however, and may frequently be the initiation point from which contextualization is sought and provided.

7. *Contract traditional musicians.* Since no teacher can know all musics, seek contractual arrangements with musicians from local ethnic-cultural communities who can teach their songs and instruments. Much like the contract violin teacher for students enrolled in the high school orchestra, traditional musicians can be hired for regularly scheduled lessons with small groups of students.

8. *Recognize that some music cannot be taught.* Certain types of religious and ceremonial music, or music of secret societies, should not be performed or even listened to. As McAllester noted, most of these musical types are not often available. But beware.

9. *Know that traditions change.* Scrutinize the recordings and publications you uncover for dates of their release, and consider that each musical work is one "moment" in the history of a people. Musical values, preferences, and attitudes change: a missionary hymn from the 1920s is no more likely to be the contemporary musical expression of the Ba-Benzele of Zaire than Tin Pan Alley music is representative of young Americans today.

10. *When in doubt, don't be afraid to*

ask your local ethnomusicologist. This advice from Waterman is worth following. Better than an on-line listserv, ethnomusicologists can give you direct answers to questions regarding traditional and contemporary musical examples, authentic performance practices, functions and values of music in cultures, media resources for instruction, and the location of culture-bearers within the community. Trust them.

Notes

1. Few of the ethnomusicologists suggested titles of the most representative songs or pieces for the culture in question. However, the lessons offer musical examples that function as "representative" music and were either suggested by the ethnomusicologist during the interview or selected by me and later approved by the ethnomusicologist.

2. Of course, in a "world music" curriculum centered on the study of musical features as they are manifested in a variety of selections, styles, and traditions, centering on an individual musical culture is not possible. See Patricia Shehan Campbell, "Music, Education, and Community in a Multicultural Society," in Marie McCarthy, ed., *Crosswinds: A Colloquium in Music Education* (College Park, MD: University of Maryland, 1996).

RESOURCE LIST

COMPILED BY EDWARD O'CONNER

There has been a steady welcome growth in the materials for teaching the musics of many of the world's cultures. This has made available a world of musical experiences for our students. As teachers, we are in a position to open the doors that lead to those experiences and to serve as guides as these young people encounter new sounds and new ways of thinking about and performing music. Much of this music has been prepared by or in conjunction with musicians and scholars from the cultures that are represented. These authorities have informed us as to what repertoire is appropriate and what performance styles are valid.

This resource list is not comprehensive, as the catalogs of distributors will demonstrate. It is a list that has been compiled from the teaching experience of ethnomusicologist/ music educators who have tried these materials with their students at the elementary, secondary, and collegiate levels and are able to provide annotations based on that experience.

The material in this resource list has been organized from the general to the specific. The initial section, **Music and Culture**, helps define the cultural context of the musical experience. It is important to view music from the perspective of any culture that is being studied and to relate music to other aspects of the culture. These books provide a framework to accomplish that.

The next section contains **Surveys of World Musics** that can give teachers a comprehensive view of people's musical experience worldwide, a basis of comparison from culture to culture, and an opportunity to grasp broad trends, both in the historical development of music and in the migration and influence of given types of music on cultures elsewhere.

The section **Textbooks for Use by Students** cites resources that may be adaptable for use in the general music class. These books have been used in college-level music classes. So far, there is no textbook designed to be read by public school students. However, the books cited here might be appropriate for secondary schools,

and teachers may adapt materials from them for other levels.

The resources in the section **Textbooks for the Teacher** are designed specifically for use in the public schools. They not only provide teachers with background information on certain cultures but include detailed lesson plans with specific materials for teaching about these cultures.

Perhaps the heart of this resource list is the section titled **Teaching Materials for Specific Cultures: With Recordings**. Here students and teachers will encounter the unique styles and nuances of performance practice that cannot necessarily be represented on the printed page. The opportunity to hear traditional performance style is critical to the success and validity of the world music experience—not only to hear it, but to begin to gain the skills to experience it through participation in performance. Many of these materials are organized in such a way as to foster successful participation at a level appropriate for various ages and grades.

In the section **Teaching Materials: Without Recordings**, some are self-explanatory and may be used with the instructions that are given. For others, teachers will want to supplement this material with recordings of other similar music from the culture until students become familiar enough with the style to perform appropriately a piece they have not heard before.

The section **Publications of the Music Educators National Conference** cites several sources designed to guide teachers in introducing the music of various cultures into the classroom. Some of these have been articles in the *Music Educators Journal*, particularly in special issues devoted to music in world cultures, while other sources have been published separately by MENC.

Scholarly journals can not only give teachers detailed insights into particular types of music throughout the world, but also provide book, recording, film, and video reviews. Some of the pertinent publications are listed in the section titled **Journals**.

Students tend to be fascinated by the way in which musical instruments have developed and migrated throughout the world and by the appearance of these instruments. Teachers also are likely to encounter the names of instruments with which they are unfamiliar in various cultures. References on **Musical Instruments** have been included that not only define and classify the instruments but also give illustrations or photographs.

Videos have become an important teaching tool, especially in those cultures where music is inseparable from dance, drama, and ritual. In fact, sometimes it can become misleading to try to present certain kinds of music out of the context of the entire event. These events are represented on videos and provide a very different kind of experience from pure listening. Also, certain videos give a good introduction to the music of a given culture because they illustrate not only what the instruments look like, but how the ensembles function, including the role of each instrument in the ensemble. From certain videos, it also is possible to learn basic dance steps.

A section on **Recording Labels** has been included. There are now available literally hundreds of recordings of world musics. It is impossible to include even a sampling of these here, but in this section are listed some of the most prominent record companies. You also will find many recordings listed in the catalogs of the distributors that follow.

Finally, some information is given on where materials may be obtained. Individual publishers have catalogs of their own publications. **Distributors** carry many of the materials in this resource list: books, sheet music and song books, recordings, videos, choral music, instrumental music, and a variety of related items from many cultures. Stay in touch with the publishers and distributors to keep up on the latest material to come onto the market.

MUSIC AND CULTURE

Campbell, Patricia Shehan. *Lessons from the World: A Cross-Cultural Guide to Music Teaching and Learning.* New York: Schirmer Books, 1991. 331 pp. Written for music educators at all levels and for choral and instrumental conductors, *Lessons from the World* examines the ways in which music is learned in various cultures throughout the world. Drawing on the work of music educators, ethnomusicologists, and learning theorists, Campbell demonstrates the importance of aural skills, and shows how observation, imitation, repetition, vocalization, solmization, and improvisation have been used in instruction throughout history and across cultures.

Kaemmer, John E. *Music in Human Life: Anthropological Perspectives on Music.* Austin: University of Texas Press, 1993. 245 pp. Cassette of musical examples.This book focuses on features of socially determined human motivation and behavior that produce music. Viewing the social ramifications of music is intended to provide a broader perspective than musicians customarily achieve when concentrating on performance. Chapters are "Sciencing" about Music; The Sociocultural Matrix: Social Factors; The Sociocultural Matrix: Conceptual Factors; Musicianship; Meaning in Music; Uses and Functions of Music; Change and Continuity; Music in Modern Life.

Lomax, Alan. *Folk Song Style and Culture.* Publication No. 88. Washington, DC: American Association for the Advancement of Science, 1968. 363 pp. Profiles are presented of the stylistic features of songs in the major cultural areas of the world with relation to other aspects of culture.

Merriam, Alan P. *The Anthropology of Music.* Evanston, IL: Northwestern University Press, 1964. 358 pp. This was the first text to define the field of ethnomusicology and remains a standard text. Particularly useful for studying the concepts of music in various cultures, such as what constitutes music, sources of music, ownership of music, optimal size of the performing group, what constitutes musical talent, and aesthetics.

Myers, Helen, ed. *Ethnomusicology: An Introduction.* New York: W. W. Norton & Company, 1992. 487 pp. Each chapter is written by an authority on that subject. Part One: Ethnomusicology; Part Two: Theory and Method (11 chapters); Part Three: Ethical Concerns and New Directions (5 chapters); Part Four: Reference Aids.

Nettl, Bruno. *The Study of Ethnomusicology: Twenty-nine Issues and Concepts.* Urbana, IL: University of Illinois Press, 1983. 410 pp. This clever collection of essays on the subject of ethnomusicology is divided into the following sections: The Comparative Study of Music, The Study of Music in Culture, The Study of Music in the Field, The Study of All of the World's Music.

Small, Christopher. *Music–Culture–Society.* New York: Schirmer Books, 1977. A philosophical examination of the role music plays in modern cultures contrasted with indigenous cultures. The author presents a strong case for a global perspective in music education.

SURVEYS OF WORLD MUSICS

Two of the following books (Nettl's *Folk and Traditional Music of the Western Continents* and Malm's *Music Cultures of the Pacific, the Near East, and Asia* are intended to be used together. They give definitions of terms appropriate for comparing musics of various cultures and provide a comprehensive worldwide survey. This would be a good starting point for teachers, who might then select specific areas to examine in greater depth. Both books include bibliography and discography. These books may be (and have been) used as the texts for a college-level course on music in world cultures.

Malm, William P. *Music Cultures of the Pacific, the Near East, and Asia.* 3rd edition. Englewood Cliffs, NJ: Prentice Hall, 1996. 236 pp. With tapes. Descriptions, music examples, and line drawings. Covers: Oceania; The Philippines, Borneo, and Indonesia; Moslem Africa, Ethiopia, and the Near East; Central and Southern Asia; Southeast Asia; East Asia; Northeast Asia and the Island Countries.

Manuel, Peter. *Popular Musics of the Non-Western World.* Oxford: Oxford University Press, 1988. 287 pp. Also: Manuel, Peter. *Cassette Culture; Popular Music and Technology in Northern India.* Chicago: University of Chicago Press, 1993. This book (which can serve as a companion book to Myers's *Ethnomusicology* explores popular musics of the world and the unprecedented means of mass dissemination. Provocative issues of ownership and power are explored.

May, Elizabeth, ed. *Musics of Many Cultures: An Introduction.* Berkeley: University of California Press, 1980. 431 pp. Includes sound sheets with some of the musical examples. Also available in paperback. This text does not give quite as comprehensive a survey as the Nettl and Malm books, but provides greater depth on various cultures. Particular chapters focus on certain aspects of music in those cultures as indicated in the chapter titles. Each chapter is by an authority on that field. This is an excellent reference work and also is suitable as a text for a college-level course on world music. Covers standard "world music" cultures and some of the lesser known cultures: Korea, Australian Aboriginal, Ethiopia, the Arabic Near East, and Eskimo (Inuit).

Myers, Helen, ed. *Ethnomusicology: Historical and Regional Studies.* New York: W. W. Norton & Company, 1993. 541 pp. This book is especially valuable as a guide to further literature, containing extensive bibliographies. With chapters by specialists, the book is divided into two principal sections. "History to World War II" covers North America (Native American, British-Americans, African-Americans, Canada); Northern and Western Europe (Germany and Austria, Switzerland, The Netherlands, France, Belgium, Iberia, Italy, Great Britain, Ireland, Scandinavia); Southern and Eastern Europe (Bulgaria, South Slavs, Poland, Bohemia, Moravia, Slovakia, Greece, Hungary, Romania); Russia, the USSR, and the Baltic States. "Regional Studies" covers Europe; Africa; West Asia; South Asia (India, Pakistan, Sri Lanka); Western Central Asia and the Caucasus; Eastern Central Asia; East Asia (China, Japan, Korea); Southeast Asia; Oceania; North America (Native American Music, African-American Music, Hispanic-American Music, British-American Folk Music, European-American, and Asian-American Music); The West Indies; and Latin America.

Nettl, Bruno. *Folk and Traditional Music of the Western Continents.* 3rd edition. Englewood Cliffs, NJ: Prentice Hall, 1990. 286 pp. Descriptions, music examples, and line drawings. Covers: Folk and Tribal Musics in Their Cultural Setting, Studying the Style of Folk Music, four chapters on European folk music, Music of Sub-Saharan Africa, The American Indians, Latin American Folk Music, Afro-American Folk Music in North and Latin America, Folk Music in Modern North America.

Olsen, Dale A. *Musics of Many Cultures: Study Guide and Workbook.* 2nd edition. Dubuque, IA: Kendall/Hunt Publishing Company, 1995. 227 pp. This is a companion to the May book (*Music of Many Cultures*). It is designed to guide students through the diverse chapters of May's textbook for college and university world music classes. The workbook will help both music and nonmusic students to more clearly understand the materials in the book; it will also aid in preparations for examinations. For each section of each chapter, the workbook gives a statement of purpose, a few paragraphs of "guidance" to the material, terms to be defined, and questions for reading comprehension. Each chapter concludes with listening exercises, sample test questions, and answers to the reading comprehension and test questions. Especially useful is a listening form with all of the elements of music defined in such a way that they can be applied to the music of any culture.

TEXTBOOKS FOR USE BY STUDENTS

Nettl, Bruno, et al. *Excursions in World Music.* Englewood Cliffs, NJ: Prentice Hall, 1992. 340 pp. A cassette of musical examples is available. Nettl does not specify a level for the book, but says of the authors' intention: "Directing ourselves to students—particularly those without a technical background in music—and to general readers, we want to show the character of music and musical life of all of the world's people." The book probably could be read without difficulty by high school students. Nettl adds: "Clearly we can [show the character of music and musical life of all of the world's people] only by sampling and by judicious synthesis, and yet we hope to go beyond the scope of other treatments of 'world music' or 'ethnic music.' Rather than considering this book only as an introduction to non-Western music, we include also the musical cultures of Europe, with its academic or art music, among the musics of the world. We divided the world into ten major culture areas or blocks, devoting a chapter to each, mindful of course that within each of these areas dwells a plethora of cultural and musical diversity. We have tried to be representative in each region of the world as well; even so, there are large areas which we have had to leave untouched." Chapters include Studying Music of the World's Cultures, India, the Middle East, China, Japan, Indonesia, Sub-Saharan Africa, Europe, Latin

America, North American Indian Music, and Old World Cultures of North America. This probably is the most accessible of the texts for use with secondary students and could be adapted for junior high level.

Titon, Jeff T. *Worlds of Music: An Introduction to the Music of the World's Peoples.* 2nd edition. New York: Schirmer Books, 1992. 469 pp. With two cassette tapes or CDs of the musical examples. Although designed for college-level courses, the book has been used for high school general music courses. The material is self-contained in that all of the musical examples in the book are on the accompanying tapes or CDs. Therefore, the book may be used without the necessity of purchasing a large number of recordings. Rather than a comprehensive survey, the text focuses on eight cultures in what is described as a case-study approach. This allows an in-depth study of each culture and its music. Transcriptions of the music examples appear in the text. A number of them could be performed by students. Particularly valuable is the last chapter which guides students in collecting ethnic music in their own communities. Each chapter is by an authority on that culture. Of special interest in each chapter is a statement by a musician from the culture on how music is learned and what the role of music is in that culture. The book is especially suitable as a textbook for a college course on teaching world musics for music education students. Chapters: The Music-Culture as a World of Music; North America/Native American; Africa/Ghana; North American/Black American; Europe/Peasant Music-Cultures of Eastern Europe; India/South India; Asia/Indonesia; East Asia/Japan; Latin America/Ecuador; Discovering and Documenting a World of Music.

TEXTBOOKS FOR THE TEACHER

The following two excellent books are designed specifically for use in the public schools. Each contains concise, authoritative information on each culture, step-by-step lesson plans, resource lists, bibliography, discography, filmography, and other sources. The George book includes suggestions for "further activities" and the Anderson/Campbell book has suggestions for integrating music with other subjects. Probably neither could be used as a text book in its entirety initially because both require the purchase of a substantial number of recordings for the musical examples and lesson plans, although a two-cassette sampler of world musics is now available for use with the Anderson/Campbell book. Teachers might start with one or two cultures and gradually build a collection of recordings. The George text does have a tape of representative pieces, but it is a small sample of the works included in the lesson plans. Nonetheless, these should be considered fundamental books for the teaching of music in world cultures.

Anderson, William M., and Patricia Shehan Campbell, eds. *Multicultural Perspectives in Music Education.* 2nd ed. Reston, VA: Music Educators National Conference, 1996. 448pp. Two-cassette sampler available. Chapters (each by an authority on the culture): Teaching Music from a Multicultural Perspective; Anglo-American; Native Americans; African American; Latin America and the Caribbean; Europe; Sub-Saharan Africa; The Middle East; South Asia: India; East Asia (China, Japan); Southeast Asia (Cambodia, Laos, Thailand, and Vietnam); and the Pacific (Oceania).

George, Luvenia A. *Teaching the Music of Six Different Cultures.* Revised and updated. Danbury, CT: World Music Press, 1987. Cassette tape. This is a book for teachers on ways of introducing students to some of the minority groups among American citizens—black, Indian, Jewish, and the many cultures represented in Hawaii. George says, "Just as I opt for presenting music *in its cultural setting* to children who are experiencing it for the first time, so as a teacher I would explore the country first, its history and mores, and then find how the music fits in, is used and constructed." Chapters: Beginning with the Elements Common to All Music; Experiences with African Music: Six Tested Lesson Plans; Teaching Black American Music; Understanding American Indian Music; Effective Strategies for Teaching Jewish Song; Studying Varieties of Hawaiian Music; Learning about Mexican and Puerto Rican Folk Music.

TEACHING MATERIALS FOR SPECIFIC CULTURES: WITH RECORDINGS

Adzinyah, Abraham K., Dumisani Maraire, and Judith Cook Tucker. *Let Your Voice Be Heard! Songs of Ghana and Zimbabwe.* Call-and-response, multipart, and game songs arranged and annotated for grades K–12. Danbury, CT: World Music Press, 1986. 116 pp. Includes a cassette tape of all songs, some sung by American school children, some by African singers, and some by both. The materials and performance style have been validated by master musicians from the cultures. Nineteen songs with transcriptions, pronunciation guide, transliteration, translation, social context, and notes on the use of each song; suggested accompaniments for clapping, bell, shakers, and drums. Chapters: Game Songs, Story Songs, Recreational Songs. Students respond enthusiastically to this material.

African Folksongs: Children's Songs from Ghana. 310 North Avenue, New Rochelle, NY 10801: Spoken Arts, Inc., 1986. 28 pp. Teacher's guide and cassette tape. There are eleven songs in the book. The accompaniments are in "highlife" style. The teacher's guide gives the lyrics, transliteration, and translation of the songs. The music must be learned aurally from the tape.

Amaoku, W. K. *African Songs and Rhythms for Children.* Orff-Schulwerk in the African Tradition. New York: Schott Music Corp., 1971. 32pp. With companion record by the same title: Folkways Records FC 7844. The book also may be obtained with an accompanying cassette. Fifteen game, cradle, speech, laments, male, mixed groups, Highlife and other songs; rhythms of the Ewe, Ghana and other peoples and languages. The score has percussion instruments. A good resource.

Ballard, Louis W. *American Indian Music for the Classroom.* 4143 North Sixteenth Street, Phoenix, AZ 85016: Canyon Records, 1973. 88 pp. Teacher's Guide, four LP records with 23 songs and dances. Separate photos, transcriptions of songs. Each song is taught on the recording phrase by phrase for pronunciation and melody by Louis Ballard, a Native American. All but two of the songs are sung by Ballard, a few with children. Ballard gives attention to stylistic differences between regions. The material is appropriate for grades 1–12, with the level indicated for each song. Songs are analyzed by form, scale, range, melody type, starting tone, secondary (mesa) tones, meter, text (vocable or meaningful text), accompaniment, grade level, learning concepts, cultural notes, and dance instructions. The material is virtually self-teaching.

Barnwell, Ysaye M., and George Brandon. *Singing in the African American Tradition: Choral and Congregational Vocal Music.* Box 694, Woodstock, NY 12498: Homespun Tapes, 1989. Six cassette tapes and a manual. Ysaye Barnwell of Sweet Honey in the Rock teaches rhythms, harmonies, vocal techniques and stylistic subtleties of the African American singing tradition. She teaches all the parts to 20 songs including chants, spirituals, early Gospel songs of the Civil Rights movement, and contemporary South African protest songs. No musical scores are presented, instead each part is taught one by one in the aural tradition. Each teaching segment is finished with a performance of all parts simultaneously. The format enables individuals, school, church, camp and community groups of any background to sing in this uplifting musical tradition. Contextual information is provided. An outstanding source for learning to perform the various styles of African American vocal music.

Brennan, Elizabeth Villarreal. "A Singing Wind: Five Melodies from Ecuador." In *Traditional Arrangements for Voices, Recorder, Guitar, Percussion, Dance, Drama, and Optional Orff Instruments.* Text and annotations in English and Spanish. Danbury, CT: World Music Press, 1988. 32 pp. Cassette tape. Suitable for various grade levels, depending on the type of activity. The manual includes transcriptions and procedures for teaching.

Burton, Bryan. *Moving within the Circle: Contemporary Native American Music and Dance.* Danbury, CT: World Music Press, 1993. 169 pp. A cassette tape includes all of the songs, performed by Native Americans. This book has been endorsed by Native American organizations. Based on field research by a Native American musician, it is authoritative and free of stereotypes. Cultural and background information is concise but thorough. There are eighteen songs to be sung and danced, five flute pieces, and six listening pieces in various contemporary styles. Song texts and vocables are given in transliteration. Chapters include Entering the Circle: Learning to Learn—Research in the Oral Tradition; Shaping the Sound: Style, Form, Substance (concepts and function, vocables, regional styles, instruments); Uniting the Circles: The Intertribal Pow-wow (definition of dance types and a description of the pow-wow); Moving within the Circle: Songs and Dances (each song is preceded by a description of where the performance was observed, what group performed it, the source of the recording, background on the type of song, and detailed dance instructions with diagrams.); Songs of the Wind: The Native American Flute (legends associated with the flute music, transcriptions to be played on recorders); A Myriad of Voices: Guided Listening Experiences (traditional, contemporary festival, contemporary fusion, American Indian Rock, concert band); Making Instruments the New Old-fashioned Way (instructions and illustrations for making dance jingles, wrist/ankle bell, rattles, drum beaters, rasps, and drums). Appendices include sources of information, advice for visiting a reservation, discography, bibliography, videos, instrument makers, craft supplies, cultural centers.

Campbell, Patricia Shehan, Ellen McCullough-Brabson, and Judith Cook Tucker. *Roots and Branches: A Legacy of Multicultural Music for Children.* Danbury, CT: World Music Press, 1994. Thirty-eight traditional songs and singing games from 23 different cultures are included for use with children ages 3 to 10. Each song is sung by a person from the culture. Selections are from Eritrea, India, Korea, Japan, Puerto Rico, Malaysia, Mozambique, Israel, Vietnam, Cambodia, Navajo, Cajun, Iran, African American, and other cultures. The book includes an overview of each culture as well as background for each song, mini-biographies of the singers, suggestions for use, map, and photos of contributors.

Canciones de mi isla—Songs from My Island. 32 Market St., New York, NY: Arts, Inc., 1981. 44 pp. Cassette tape. There are brief explanations of some of these Puerto Rican songs. Includes 14 folk and children's songs and 5 adult songs. The recordings are valid in vocal performance style although the instrumental accompaniments are not altogether traditional. The pitches of the transcriptions do not always match the recording. Harmony lines and some verses are omitted. Not all of the songs occur in the same order on the tape as in the book. Nonetheless, this is a usable source for learning the songs and the Spanish texts.

De Cesare, Ruth, ed. *Songs of Hispanic Americans.* An Educator's Resource Book of Folk Songs from the Mexican-American Border, the American Southwest, and Puerto Rico. P.O. Box 10003, 16380 Roscoe Blvd., Van Nuys, CA 91410-0003: Alfred Publishing Co., 1991. Cassette tape. This book was designed for the classroom teacher, social science, and Spanish language instructors, as well as music specialists from the primary through middle school grades. Featured are 27 songs, each prefaced with background information. The Teacher's Resource Book indicates the complexity of each song by general grading into three levels: A, B, and C. Music experiences include singing in Spanish and English, performance of a variety of syncopated rhythm patterns, and participating in a graded program of part-singing in thirds and sixths. Movement and game playing are included for younger students. Autoharp and guitar chording is provided for every song.

Floyd, Leela. *Indian Music.* London: Oxford University Press, 1980. 48 pp. Cassette tape. Part of the "Oxford Topics in Music" series, the manual states: "These short, illustrated books are designed to explore a range of musical topics of interest to 11–14 year olds. Since reading and fact-gathering should never be a substitute for listening to or playing music, a number of suggestions for practical work are included, though in some cases these may be only the starting point for the musical work that could be related to a particular topic." Chapters: India and its culture; Five kinds of music; The form of Indian music; Instruments and their players; The history of Indian music. The material is much more sketchy than Shankar's *Learning India Music*, but it might be a good starting point.

Fukuda, Hanako. *Favorite Songs of Japanese Children.* 14751 Carmenita Road, Norwalk, CA 90650: Highland Music Company, 1965. 25 pp. Cassette tape. Teachers who are looking for song material that will help them to better understand people will welcome this collection of Japanese songs. Fukuda's wide background of teaching in Japanese schools, and her firsthand knowledge of American children and music as taught in American schools, gives the book an authenticity and usefulness that is unique. The informative notes about the songs help to build a background of understanding the people of Japan. The suggestions for enriching the songs with appropriate instruments make it possible for the teacher to create a background of sound and movement that will sound Japanese, but will also be understandable and enjoyable to American children. Dance or game instructions and formations are given for some of the songs. Japanese singing currently occurs in two styles: the rather tight, closed-throat traditional style and the more relaxed, open, contemporary Western-based style that is commonly taught in Japanese schools. The performances on the tape are in the Western style and provide a valid model for American children.

Han Kuo-Huang, and Patricia Shehan Campbell. *The Lion's Roar: Chinese Luogu Percussion Ensembles.* Danbury, CT: World Music Press, 1992. 69 pp. The accompanying tape includes all selections. The text contains short background sections on China and its musical traditions. The percussion selections contain mnemonic chants with pronunciation guides, a condensed score of the overall "conglomerate" rhythms, and a score of the individual parts. Seven selections employ pure, nonpitched percussion, and four include melody that can be played with Western melodic instruments with limited percussion accompaniment to illustrate the possibilities of Western classroom adaptation.

Harpole, Patricia, and Mark Fogelquist. *Los Mariachis! An Introduction to Mexican Mariachi Music.* Danbury, CT: World Music Press, 1989. 20 pp. Cassette tape. This is essentially a guided listening lesson for the *son* "El Tirador." Each instrumental part in the ensemble is illustrated. Also included are complete examples of the song types: *son*, polka, waltz, ranchera, and bolero. An excellent, clearly illustrated, and enjoyable resource.

Jessup, Lynne. *The Mandinka Balafon: An Introduction with Notation for Teaching.* New York: Magnum Music, 1985. 191 pp. With two tapes, the first containing the pieces to be performed by students, and the second containing complex pieces by master musicians for listening. The balafon is a xylophone of the Mandinka people of Gambia, West Africa. Orff xylophones can be adapted to play this music. The first three chapters give detailed notes on the instrument and its cultural context, analysis of the music, and methods of teaching the balafon. Chapter 4 contains transcriptions of 18 pieces that students can perform. Some of the songs have texts that can be sung. The balafon pieces are taught on the tape with hands alone and then together.

Jones, Bessie, and Bess Lomax Hawes. *Step It Down: Games, Plays, Songs, and Stories from the Afro-American Heritage.* Athens, Georgia: University of Georgia Press, 1987. 233 pp. Cassette tape by the same title. Rounder Records, One Camp Street, Cambridge, MA 02140. The book includes notes to parents and teachers, description of the context and manner of performing each song, bibliography, discography. The recording is especially important for getting a sense of elements of performance style that cannot be notated. Eighteen of the songs are on the tape. A separate booklet accompanies the tape. The material has proven to be very effective in the classroom and may be used with lower elementary students.

Kazadi wa Mukuna. *African Children's Songs for American Elementary Schools.* East Lansing, MI: African Studies Center and Music Department, Michigan State University, 1979. 40 pp. Cassette tape of the songs accompanies the text. This text contains 10 songs with pronunciation guides, and a section on making African rhythm instruments for use in the classroom. Though currently out of print, this text can be obtained directly from Dr. wa Mukuna at the Hugh A. Glauser School of Music, Kent State University, Kent OH 44242-0001. The songs were tested in Michigan public schools, and the accompanying cassette tape is a recording of these students in performance. Song texts are read aloud before each selection to assist with pronunciation.

Locke, David. *Drum Gahu: A Systematic Method for an African Percussion Piece.* Crown Point, IN: White Cliffs Media Company, 1987. Cassette tape. A comprehensive approach to learning the rhythms of a percussion piece, primarily for advanced players but useful for anyone who wishes to know how the percussion ensemble functions.

Mattox, Cheryl Warren. *Shake It to the One That You Love the Best: Play Songs and Lullabies from Black Musical Traditions.* 3817 San Pablo Dam Rd., #336, El Sobrante, CA 94803: Warren-Mattox Productions, 1989. 56 pp. Cassette tape. The book contains 16 play songs and 10 lullabies. While all of the songs in this book have become part of the treasured musical traditions of Black cultures, their popularity often transcends cultural boundaries. But in cases where the songs are embraced by those outside the Black tradition, there sometimes are marked differences in the melody, rhythm, lyrics, and game action. The same holds true in instances where the songs may have origins elsewhere and were adopted by Black cultures. Each selected song carries a notation indicating the culture most closely associated with the 'treatment' presented. The lullabies often have soothing melodies and promises of special treats in an effort to lull a child to sleep. The play songs are companions to children's games and fall into three categories. Ring games are played in a circle formation, sometimes with a child designated to perform a special role standing in the center. In line games, participants form two lines, often pairing up to dance or complete other motions together. And with clapping rhymes, players can get as intricate as they like in creating rhythmic patterns to accompany the words. The songs are recorded in a contemporary jazz style.

McLaughlin, Roberta. *Folk Songs of Africa.* 1311 North Highland Ave., Hollywood, CA 90028: Highland Music Company, 1963. 17 pp. The accompanying recording, which was out of print, is coming back into print. The book contains sixteen songs, primarily from countries of central Africa. The songs are appropriate for lower elementary grades and up. Both unison and part-songs are included. Some have African texts only; some English texts only; some have both. There is a one-page general introduction, then very brief comments on some of the songs. However, there is very little information on the cultural context. The recording is important for learning appropriate tempos and, to some extent, style. However, it would be well to supplement with recordings of traditional African performances from these countries. While the performances on this recording are by African musicians, there is a distinct "English" manner to the style.

Nguyen, Phong Thuyet, and Patricia Shehan Campbell. *From Rice Paddies and Temple Yards: Traditional Music of Vietnam.* Danbury, CT: World Music Press, 1990. 88 pp. Cassette tape. An extremely varied collection that includes game songs, love songs, boating songs, recited and sung poetry, and instrumental music. It offers a section on the history and culture of Vietnam, a general introduction to the music and instruments, and twelve vocal and instrumental pieces with study guides for group use. Appropriate and absorbing for readers and listeners of all ages and grade levels. The professional companion tape is by a group of Vietnamese musicians currently living in the United States.

Nyberg, Anders. *Freedom Is Coming.* Songs of Protest and Praise from South Africa for mixed choir. P.O. Box 470, Chapel Hill, NC 27514: Walton Music Corporation, 1984. 38 pp. With cassette tape. All fifteen pieces are performed on the tape both in English and in the Zulu, Xhota, or Sotho languages. A pronunciation guide is provided. The songs may be sung unaccompanied or with rhythm instruments. Although written for SATB, they also are designed to be sung in a variety of other arrangements, including two-part for children. Excellent for high school choir, students find this music to be very appealing. The recording is by a Swedish group, but South African musicians have indicated that the performance style is appropriate.

Paz, Elena. *Songs in Spanish for Children.* Columbia Special Products. Stereo 91A-02029. This recording contains 14 songs with an accompanying sheet with the texts and translations. This is a fine resource in terms of style, and especially in terms of pronunciation of the Spanish texts in that it is intended primarily to enhance language instruction. Each song is designed to help in learning vocabulary, pronunciation, idioms, linking of words in speech, and patterns of speech. The album contains songs about days of the week, weather, birthdays, seasons, marketing, party games, and Christmas carols.

Peña, Manuel. *The Texas-Mexican Conjunto: History of a Working-Class Music.* Austin, TX: University of Texas Press, 1985. Companion recording by the same title, Folklyric Records #9049 (long play record), available from Down Home Music/Arhoolie Records, 10341 San Pablo Avenue, El Cerrito, CA 94350. This is the best book available on the subject of the accordion-led music of southern Texas.

Sam, Sam-Ang, and Patricia Shehan Campbell. *Silent Temples, Songful Hearts: Traditional Music of Cambodia.* Danbury, CT: World Music Press, 1991. 144 pp. Cassette tape. Featuring personal comments by Sam-Ang Sam on each selection, the book includes a wide variety of songs and instrumental pieces, from children's lilting etiquette songs, game songs and dances to drum, xylophone and flute pieces, and exciting boxing music and stories told through song and narration. Introductory chapters focus on the history and geography of Cambodia, (including the terrible period of the genocidal Pol Pot and the Khmer Rouge), customs and traditions, and instruments and musical styles. Fourteen lessons explore seventeen musical selections and include musical transcriptions, the words to all songs in Khmer with English translation, extensive background information, and a Study Guide including a separate section for the music professional. The professionally produced companion tape features Sam-Ang Sam, his daughters, and other musicians currently living in the United States. The appropriate grade levels are indicated for each piece, from early childhood through adult.

Serwadda, W. Moses. *Songs and Stories from Uganda.* New York: Thomas Y. Crowell, 1974. 80 pp. Available with cassette tape. Thirteen songs with stories, pronunciation guide, translations (however, to be sung in the original language), some with accompaniment of clapping, bell, rattle, drums. Performance on the tape by

Ugandan musicians. A very good and usable resource.

Shankar, Ravi. *Learning Indian Music: A Systematic Approach.* Elise B. Barnett, ed. 170 N.E. 33rd Street, Ft. Lauderdale, FL 33334: Onomatopoeia, Inc., 1979. Manual, 76 pp. Three cassette tapes. Shankar leads a class through a series of exercises and songs to introduce the concepts and skills of North Indian music. It is a thorough, step-by-step approach, including definition of terms, illustration, and experiences with a variety of ragas and talas, the Indian solfège system, ornamentation, and improvisation. Students are able to sing along with the tapes. An excellent source to introduce the music of India through participation.

Tanna, Laura. *Jamaican Folk Tales and Oral Histories.* No. 1, Jamaica 21 Anthology Series. 2A Suthermere Road, Kingston 10, Jamaica: Institute of Jamaica Publications, 1988. 143 pp. Companion tape with eleven of the examples. More than sixty oral histories, songs, rhymes, riddles, proverbs, narratives, and stories. Thoroughly documented. Some of the stories have songs in them; others do not. Students would enjoy learning the dialect to tell and sing the stories.

Thrasher, Alan R. *La-Li-Luo Dance-Songs of the Chuxiong Yi, Yunnan Province, China.* Danbury, CT: World Music Press, 1990. 141 pp. Cassette tape. Based on a dissertation, this book features a thorough description of the cultural context of dance-songs of one of the minority groups of China. The dance patterns are described, and thirteen songs are included with the dance steps indicated in the score. Four additional songs are included without dance steps. A number of the dances have texts or vocables (there is a pronunciation guide) and would be suitable for performance by students of various grade levels. The tape includes both field recordings and studio recordings. Chapters include The Setting; Cultural Background; The Dance-Song and its Performance Context; Musical Instruments; Dance (formation, dance steps, dance patterns, tempos and moods); Music: Texture, Mode, and Melodic Structure; Music: Vocables and Song Texts; Conclusion: Status of Preservation.

Wilson, Chesley Goseyun, Ruth Longcor Harnisch Wilson, and Bryan Burton. *When the Earth Was Like New: Western Apache Songs and Stories.* Danbury, CT: World Music Press, 1994. Cassette tape or CD. The collection includes 17 musical transcriptions of social, traveling, and game songs and Apache violin pieces; 38 archival and contemporary photographs of instruments, ceremonies, and social life; fully illustrated instructions for making and decorating the Apache violin; historical and cultural background about the Apache in general as well as the Wilson family; complete background about each song, most of which has never been published; traditional legends.

TEACHING MATERIALS: WITHOUT RECORDINGS

Ajibola, J. O. *Yoruba Songs.* 2nd ed. Ile-Ife, Nigeria: University of Ife Press, 1974. This book consists of 38 sacred songs and 34 secular songs, all in staff notation in one, two, three, or four parts with piano accompaniment.

Alevizos, Susan and Ted. *Folk Songs of Greece.* New York: Oak Publications, 1968. 96 pp. Distributed by Music Sales.

Jessup, Lynn. *Afro Ensemble: A Beginning Book.* PO Box 1356, Ft. Worth, TX 76101: Harris Music Publications, 1975. 26 pp. Seven rhythmic patterns for percussion ensemble. May be done with standard classroom and orchestral or African percussion instruments. Introduces students to the structure of the African ensemble through simple box notation and relatively uncomplicated rhythmic patterns.

PUBLICATIONS OF THE MUSIC EDUCATORS NATIONAL CONFERENCE

Anderson, William M., and Patricia Shehan Campbell, eds. *Multicultural Perspectives in Music Education.* 2nd ed. Reston, VA: MENC, 1996. (See description under Textbooks for the Teacher.)

Becoming Human through Music. The Wesleyan Symposium on the Perspectives of Social Anthropology in the Teaching and Learning of Music. David McAllester, ed. Reston, VA: MENC, 1985. 134 pp. This publication contains the papers from The Wesleyan Symposium. Not a "how-to" book, the material is useful in developing concepts of music in culture as related to education.

Bringing Multicultural Music to Children. Video. Reston, VA: MENC, 1992. In this video, drawn from presentations at MENC conferences and symposia, five noted music professors present innovative ways to teach young students about the music of other cultures. Included are songs and chants from Africa, China, and Jamaica; and music from Native Americans, African Americans, and the Maori of New Zealand. The video features good demonstrations of lessons. Unfortunately, there is no printed version of the songs for teachers to use in the classroom.

Music Educators Journal. The following issues of the *MEJ* had "special focus" themes and introduced the musics of a variety of cultures with suggestions for teaching approaches, bibliography, and so forth. The articles in each issue were necessarily brief but offered further resources: Music in World Cultures, October, 1972; Improvisation, January, 1980 (including improvisation in Latin American, West African, Near Eastern, and Korean music); The Multicultural Imperative, May, 1983; and Multicultural Music Education, May, 1992.

Music Resources for Multicultural Perspectives. Audiocassette. Reston, VA: MENC, 1995. This two-cassette sampler of world musics features music from North America, Latin America and the Caribbean, Europe, Sub-Saharan Africa, the Middle East, South Asia, East Asia, and Southeast Asia. It can be used in conjunction with the text *Multicultural Perspectives in Music Education.*

Sounds of the World. A series of recordings on world musics. Reston, VA: MENC, 1986–1990. Publications in the *Sounds of the World* series consist of two elements: high-quality stereo cassettes containing narration, interviews, and music examples, and an accompanying illustrated teacher's guide with background information, pictures of instruments, and suggestions for using these materials with elementary, secondary, and college-level students. Some of the musical examples can be performed by students; most are for listening. Each packet contains three cassettes. The series includes *Music of Eastern Europe: Albanian, Greek, and South Slavic; Music of Southeast Asia: Lao, Hmong, Vietnamese; Music of the Middle East: Arab, Persian/Iranian, and Turkish; Music of East Asia: China, Korea, Japan;* and *Music of Latin America: Mexico, Ecuador, Brazil.*

Teaching Music with a Multicultural Approach. A set of four videos and a book. Reston, VA: MENC, 1991. This collection of videos and the accompanying book are taken from the 1990 Symposium on Multicultural Approaches in Music Education, an event that received rave review from all who attended. The highlights of the symposium are the focus of this collection, exploring the history and philosophy of music from different cultural groups and providing practical teaching ideas and examples for use in the classroom. Each cassette features one of four cultures: African Americans, Asian Americans, Hispanic Americans, and American Indians. The book features music examples, lesson plans, and resource lists for teaching the music of these cultures. MENC cautions that the videos, themselves, are not designed for classroom use; rather, they are a resource for teachers.

JOURNALS

Ethnomusicology. Journal of the Society for Ethnomusicology. Business office: Morrison Hall 005, Indiana University, Bloomington, IN 47405. Articles, bibliography, discography, filmography, book reviews.

Sing Out! 125 East Third Street, PO Box 5253, Bethlehem, PA 18015-0253 (Tel: 215/865-5344). A folk song magazine that contains songs, articles on performers, columns, reviews, and festival listings. The corporation provides songs search and maintains an archive and resource center. Recent recording projects are geared to children.

The World of Music. Journal of the International Institute for Traditional Music. Florian Noetzel Edition, PO Box 580, D 26353 Wilhelmshaven, Germany. The journal focuses on the diverse musical traditions and arts of the world.

MUSICAL INSTRUMENTS

Ardley, Neil. *Music.* Eyewitness Books. New York: Alfred A. Knopf, 1989. A resource for the elementary classroom. Hundreds of photographs of musical instruments, many from world musics.

Blackwood, Alan. *Music: The Illustrated Guide to Music around the World from its Origins to the Present Day.* London: Mallard Press, 1991. 256 pp. A picture book that incorporates photographs with diagrams and text. It includes world music.

Boulton, Laura. *Musical Instruments of World Cultures.* New York: Intercultural Arts Press, 1975. Pictures, line drawings, and descriptions of instruments from world musics contained in the Laura Bolton Collection at Arizona State University.

Buchner, Alexander. *Folk Music Instruments.* New York: Crown Publishers, 1972. This is a fine "picture book" of selected instruments from around the world. The photographs are excellent.

Marcuse, Sibyl. *Musical Instruments: A Comprehensive Dictionary.* New York: W. W. Norton & Co., 1975. 608 pp. Terms for instruments may be encountered, especially on recordings, where the type of instrument is not identified. This is an excellent reference book for that purpose.

Musical Instruments of the World: An Illustrated Encyclopedia. New York: Facts on File Publications, 1976. 320 pp. This is a particularly valuable resource for class use, not only for pictures of instruments, but for the classification system of instruments; for illustrations of folk, historical, and modern instruments; and for comparison of families of instruments from one culture to another. More than 4000 original drawings.

Sadie, Stanley, ed. *The New Grove Dictionary of Musical Instruments.* London: Macmillan Press, 1984. Contains detailed information about musical instruments. The user must know the name of the instrument in order to use this reference effectively.

Walther, Tom. *Make Mine Music!* Boston: Little Brown and Company, 1981. A resource for the elementary classroom on the making of simple musical instruments, many patterned after instruments from world musics.

Waring, Dennis. *Making Wood Folk Instruments.* 387 Park Ave. South, New York, NY 10016: Sterling Publishing Co., 1990. Intended for school children. The instruments are substantial, not toys.

VIDEOS

The American Indian Dance Theatre (order through distributors). *Finding the Circle* is a one-hour program from PBS featuring dances from a variety of Native American communities and commentary on the culture. Authentic in style with professional Native American dancers.

Bock, Richard. *India's Master Musicians.* Los Angeles: Aura Productions, 1982. This film/video includes performances by Imrat Khan, Lakshmi Shankar, Ashish Khan, Alla Rakha, Lakshmi Viswanathan, Zakir Hussain, and Ramanad Raghavan.

The Dennis Alley Wisdom Dancers, PO Box 33053, Phoenix, AZ 85067, (602) 973-2026. *Wisdom Dancers* is a 30-minute introduction to Native American dances, several featuring young people as the dancers.

Dove Music (distributor), PO Box 08286, Milwaukee, WI 53208. *Beats of the Heart* is a documentary video series by Jeremy Marre that addresses social implications and dynamics of a variety of traditional and popular musics. Each video is 60 minutes, including such topics as Indian cinema music, New York salsa, and gypsies in Europe and Asia.

Educational Video, 1401 19th St., Huntsville, TX 77340. Available videos include *Music of Japan, Music of Latin America, Mexican American Musical Heritage, Sounds of Mexico, Music of India, Music of Africa*, and *Russian Folk Music.* Each video is 20-22 minutes.

Haydon, Geoffrey, and Dennis Marks. *Repercussion—A Celebration of African-American Music.* Chicago: A Third Eye Production for RM Arts Home Vision, 1984. This series includes seven one-hour documentary films on four video cassettes: Program 1: *Born Musicians—Traditional Music from Gambia;* Program 2: *On the Battlefield—Gospel Quartets;* Program 3: *Legends of Rhythm and Blues;* Program 4: *Sit Down and Listen—The Story of Max Roach;* Program 5: *The Drums of Dagbon;* Program 6: *Caribbean Crucible;* and Program 7: *Africa Come Back—The Popular Music of West Africa.*

Holender, Jacques. *Kodo—Heartbeat Drummers of Japan.* New York: Rhapsody Films, 1983. 58 minutes. The film showcases Kodo's music and explores the performers' commitment to a unique aesthetic and collective ideal.

Homespun Tapes, PO Box 694, Woodstock, NY 12498-0694, 800-338-2737. These tapes offer music lessons on traditional instruments, including guitar, banjo, and fiddle as well as yodeling, Andean pipes, and African-American singing.

Interworld Music, 139 Noriega Street, San Francisco, CA 94122, (415) 242-9788, fax: (415) 242-9789. *The Essence of Percussion* includes instructional tapes in jazz and contemporary genres as well as Latin-based Congas, Irish bodhran and bones, and African Djembe drumming.

Multicultural Media (distributor), R.R. 3, Box 6655, Granger Rd., Barre, VT 05641.The *VC Video Anthology of World Music and Dance* offers thirty videos with nine books of background information (more than 100 countries and over 500 performances are presented). This is an especially valuable set for showing music in relation to dance, drama, and ritual. Instrumental music also is represented in its performance setting. Although the quality is not even throughout the set, there is more than enough good material for classroom use. It would be an excellent library resource not only for music teachers, but also for teachers in other fields.

Oklahoma University Foundation/Early Music Television, School of Music, Eugene Enrico, Director, University of Oklahoma, Norman, OK 73019. The videos *Gagaku, Ancient Japanese Court Music and Dance* and *Bunraku, Japanese Puppet Theatre* include detailed explanations.

Shankar, Ravi. *Raga.* New York: Mystic Fire Video, 1991. 141 minutes. This video explores Ravi Shankar's musical, cultural and spiritual roots. This intimate portrait follows Shankar rehearsing, teaching, and performing in concert.

Solaris Lakota, 264 W. 19th St., New York, NY 10011, (212) 741-0778. *Live and Remember* is a 30-minute explanation of Lakota (Sioux) world view and other aspects of culture with demonstrations of the role of music and dance. An outstanding tape to introduce students to Native American culture, produced by members of the Lakota nation.

Sukay. *How to Play Flutes of the Andes.* Woodstock, NY: Homespun Tapes, 1987. Quentin Howard and Carlos Crespo demonstrate the fine points of performing on the zampona and kena.

RECORDING LABELS

Arhoolie Records, 10341 San Pablo Avenue, El Cerrito, CA 94350 (Tex-Mex and Cajun music).

Canyon Records and Indian Arts, 4143 North 16th Avenue, Phoenix, AZ 85016 (Native American music).

Lyrichord Discs, Inc., 141 Perry Street, New York, NY 10014.

Nonesuch Records, 590 Fifth Ave., New York, NY 10036, (212) 575-6720.

Smithsonian/Folkways Records, Office of Folklife Programs, 955 L'Enfant Plaza, Suite 2600, Smithsonian Institution, Washington, DC 20560.

DISTRIBUTORS

Many of the teaching resources listed above may be obtained from the following distributors. Write for their catalogs.

About Music: A Catalog. Audio-Forum, 96 Broad Street, Guilford, CT 06437, 800-243-1234.
Audio and video cassettes, song books. Note especially the video series by Deben Bhattacharya on music and dance, religion and social customs, and arts and crafts related to the everyday life of people in many countries of Asia (each 30 minutes), as well as the LP, cassette, or CD collection for *Ethnic Music from around the World.*

Dove Music, PO Box 08286, Milwaukee, WI 53208, (414) 444-4447; fax: (414) 444-4485.

Multicultural Media, R.R. 3, Box 6655, Granger Rd., Barre, VT 05641, (802) 223-1294; fax: (802) 229-1834; order department: 800-550-9675.

Music in Motion, 783 North Grove #108, Richardson, TX 75081, 800-445-0649.

West Music Company, 1208 Fifth Street, PO Box 5521, Coralville, IA 52241, 800-397-9378; fax 319-351-9318.

World Music Institute Catalog: *Music from around the World.* 49 W. 27th St., Suite 810, New York, NY 10001, (212) 545-7536. (CDs, cassettes, videotapes, books.)